MW00935550

BIBLES AND BRIEFCASES

BIBLES AND BRIEFCASES

A Biblical Economic Guide for the Believer in Business

Rodney Dale Swope

Copyright © 2017 by Rodney Dale Swope.

ISBN: Softcover   978-1-5245-8090-2
             Ebook   978-1-5245-8091-9

All rights reserved. No part of this book may be reproduced or transmitted in any form or by any means, electronic or mechanical, including photocopying, recording, or by any information storage and retrieval system, without permission in writing from the copyright owner.

KJV
Scripture quotations marked KJV are from the Holy Bible, King James Version (Authorized Version). First published in 1611. Quoted from the KJV Classic Reference Bible, Copyright © 1983 by The Zondervan Corporation.

NIV
All Scripture quotations, unless otherwise indicated are taken from the *Holy Bible New, International Version*®. NIV®. Copyright © 1973, 1978, 1984 by International Bible Society. Used by permission of Zondervan. All rights reserved. [Biblica]

AMP
Scripture quotations marked AMP are from *The Amplified Bible,* Old Testament copyright © 1965, 1987 by the Zondervan Corporation. *The Amplified Bible,* New Testament copyright © 1954, 1958, 1987 by The Lockman Foundation. Used by permission. All rights reserved.

Any people depicted in stock imagery provided by Thinkstock are models, and such images are being used for illustrative purposes only.
Certain stock imagery © Thinkstock.

Print information available on the last page.

Rev. date: 02/17/2017

To order additional copies of this book, contact:
Xlibris
1-888-795-4274
www.Xlibris.com
Orders@Xlibris.com
626997

This book is dedicated to my circle of relations who have shaped who I am, stimulated my pursuit of knowledge, and fueled my achievements through prayer and encouragement, and to the ever more present marketplace ministers striving to fulfill divine calling.

Contents

Foreword

Believers who are truly committed to living out the Kingdom principles that are prescribed in the Bible are constantly on a mission to make the word of God practical. They are determined to actually discover the ways in which they can cause their behavior to emulate the expectations as well as the privileges outlined in the Holy Scriptures. For the genuine believer in the Lord Jesus Christ, theirs is not simply lip service to what it means to be a disciple. Theirs is a strong desire to be what it is that they read. The genuine believers want to ensure that their lives are so closely aligned with the Word of God that there is no dissimulation, there is no duality between their lives and the Word. It is this sincere desire on the part of believers in Jesus Christ to be authentic that is tremendously accomplished through Rodney Swope's text.

What we find in Rodney Swope's *Bibles and Briefcases* is a blend of the excavation of the Word of God and the strategies to implement, in our everyday lives, both the expectations and the privileges we possess as believers in Jesus Christ. This text unashamedly requires the reader to come to grips with some fundamental principles of economics. It is very comforting, however, to realize that the components of this groundbreaking text that unearths for the reader these foundational tenets of economics are not hard to grasp especially for one who is not familiar with theories and principles of either micro or macroeconomics. What Rodney does, in this text, is to subsume what might be difficult principles, for the lay person to wrap his/her mind around, in the greater context of what the word of God says about finances, the Lord's role in sustaining the believers' place of prominence in matters of economics and finances and the privileges those who are in the Kingdom of God receive simply because of their divine citizenship.

Another phenomenal aspect of this work is the fact that the reader is given, the opportunity to reflect and to take personal steps to implement the content of this text. Questions at the end of the chapter such as, if your household is an economic system what are the means of trade, what do you give and what do you get in exchange and how are you sowing your life in a way that produces value for the Kingdom of God and make a holiday spending plan are all parts of this book that cause the reader not only to think but to also take pragmatic steps to engage personally the words of this text. This undoubtedly helps the reader to move what is found in *Bibles and Briefcases* from the realm of theory into practice.

Additionally, the reader will be exposed to both the Old and New Testament scriptures that undergird Swope's conceptualization of biblical economics. I have been impressed that within the pages of this book are biblical frames that allow the believer who serves as a businessperson to be comfortable in engaging in lucrative financial enterprises while concomitantly living as a committed believer in Jesus Christ. Rodney Swope requires the believer to not only embrace the word of the Lord found in both canons of the scriptures but to also see themselves as creators who have the authority and the privilege as he writes to, "create by speaking it into your business, your ministry or your life".

Bibles and Briefcases comes at a very significant time in the life of the Kingdom of God. It is a must read for those who want to take the next proactive steps in living out the principles of biblical economics in a studied way as opposed to one contextualized in hype and misinformation. I definitely applaud the deep biblical exegesis as well as the call for practical application that this book presents.

Bishop Michael E. Dantley
Christ Emmanuel Christian Fellowship
Cincinnati, Ohio

Preface

This book is written to Christians in the marketplace. I refer to them as "believers in business." While this distinction could include every Christian, for we are all buyers or sellers in the marketplace, let us further segment this group to those leading in business. Whether you are an employee, entrepreneur, intre-preneur, or social enterprise manager, if you are a person with an earnest desire to apply the Word of God at work, this guide is for you.

> "The marketplace- a synthesis of business, education and government- is to a metropolis what the heart is to the human body. Through these three arteries flows the life of a city. A city cannot exist without a marketplace in the same fashion that a body cannot exist without a heart."
>
> Ed Silvoso, "Annointed for Business", pg 16

I am a believer in business. I often say I am a marketplace minister disguised as an economic developer and business coach. I get out of bed, pray, read, stretch a little, dress, eat, and drive to the office like every other Christ follower working in a secular job. Yet, many years ago I decided to see my job as tour of duty serving the Kingdom of God. In the places I go for work I might be the only Jesus they see. Can I be a good and godly man at work? Of course! especially if I seek the face of the CEO of the universe, invite him into my daily affairs, and remain conscious of kingdom work while I'm walking and talking in the marketplace. I am persuaded that some of us are called to serve as minsters in the marketplace.

At the turn of the century I was a mid-level executive in the supply chain discipline of a fortune 100 company and the assistant pastor of new and promising, progressive Bible believing full gospel church plant. I was reading the Bible cover to cover in many of those years. I was also inspired by prophets like John Maxwell, Ron Blue, Ed Silvosa, and Stephen Covey, and others who were all building bridges between the faith and business sectors. Even the White House had found some common ground between government and the faith community as the White House Office of Faith-Based and Community Initiatives was established by executive order in 2001. I was trying to figure out how to be a Christian at work. I was that religious guy who didn't drink alcohol at business dinners nor tolerate profanity in my office. These prophets were espousing a Christian point of view on ordinary business topics like leadership, finances, economics, and management. Their messages were crossing over and becoming core reading for enlightened business readers everywhere. I became a voracious reader and astute follower of these writers.

At the same time the church was teaching the kingdom of God, how it works and how to appropriate the John 10:10 abundant life. I began to sense a convergence of these two economies—the world and the kingdom. I became hungry for more knowledge about the kingdom economy. I was certain it was more than tithes, offerings, and first fruits. I wondered what was the framework and wiring for the kingdom economy. How does it work?

To understand a kingdom, I thought, a business framework is not enough. While business is a part of how a nation or kingdom operates, clearly a kingdom is not a business. Nations and kingdoms do however have economies, and all the local and regional economies aggregate to the national or kingdom economy. I concluded that economics was a far better framework to understand the whole. Well, lots can be found and read about economics, but I wondered, what does the Bible say about economics? Economics is the study of production, distribution, and consumption. The Bible must say something about making things, moving things around, and using things up. I liked the idea of studying about economics in general, but learning about biblical economics lit an unquenchable thirst for knowledge and wisdom on the subject.

I learned that the word *economics*, which is *okionomos* in the Greek, is derived from two words: *Okios*, meaning house, and *nomos*, meaning law. Hence the economics is interpreted the "law of the house." This resonated with me. I had become a student of business law, and kingdom of God laws. So the notion of laws was clear to me. To discover there were also laws of the house, a household or even the house of God was a profound revelation that made economics a simpler and more essential body of knowledge that intrigued me to pursue a deeper understanding.

So after nearly twenty years for seeking, knocking, and asking, I put some of what I've learned in this book. My journey goes on. Please join me in review some of the Biblical economic ideas I have discovered so far.

Introduction

The walls are crumbling and the lines blurred between life for the Christ follower and his or her career in business. Practically every barrier has been challenged in the decades surrounding the start of the new millennium. We have seen government sponsored faith-based initiatives, pastors in politics, and for profit social services from hospices to drug rehabs. We have even seen a nonprofit bank become a world leader of micro loans in developing countries. Economy is becoming increasingly ecumenical. It includes local and global, religious and secular, as well as church and state. The lines of demarcation that once kept us all in our lanes have morphed into a complex web of open networks.

We have become dichotomous beings living a duality of opposing worlds. Many of us attempt to live in two worlds while often feeling inadequate in both.

- We are in the world, but not of the world.
- We are saints and sinners.
- We are rich with hope and poor in spirit.
- We are masters of business and ministers in the church.

The world we live is constantly driving a psychological wedge between what we confess to believe and what we consider our daily reality.

It's prompting us to separate

- church and state;
- friends and family from clients and business associates;

- work from worship;
- marriage from ministry;
- beliefs from business; and
- faith from finances.

While so many economic elements have found the "genius of and," the typical believer in business is still suffering from the polar dysfunction of separating faith from finances in the same way many have sought to impugn faith's influence on our government under the guise of separation of church and state. Our mostly Christian constitutional founders never meant that our faith should not influence government, but that government should not interfere with one's freedom of religion. As Alexis De Tocqueville so aptly put, "despotism can govern without faith, but liberty cannot." While business must not interfere with the affairs of the church, our faith must influence the way we conduct business.

With a fervent traditionalism, we have guarded the code of politeness by never mixing bread and blessings, government and grace, nor the Great Commission and commerce. These formerly fortified walls of demarcation have kept many of us paralyzed to share our faith in the marketplace—the one place that we spend most of our time with pre-Christians. Our beliefs are in the Bible, our business in our briefcases. Without a new paradigm, never the twain shall meet.

The protectors of the status quo say, "Don't bring that religious stuff to the office" and "Please keep that corporate stuff out of my church; it's all about faith here."

We cannot be successful in the rapidly shrinking world if we continue to attempt to separate our faith from our work. It is not the time to separate but to integrate. The world needs the truth. Believers in business are in the best position to shake hands, break bread, and build relationships with those needing Christ. This message is not about traditional evangelism, but perhaps a simple and yet radical evangelism that commands us to fulfill the Great Commission while we do our work. We cannot leave our faith and the power of the Kingdom of God at home while we go off to work. *Bible and Briefcases* offers principles and tips to remain congruent with your beliefs while succeeding in your business.

1

What Is Biblical Economics?

The purpose of the economic order is to provide a standard of living that not only meets people's basic physical needs (such as food, clothing, shelter and medical care) but also facilitates their pursuit of higher values, including the highest value of all, the ultimate goal of union with God.

J. Michael Stebbins

"Biblical economics" is a phrase that often raises eyebrows when spoken. Can these two words share the same sentence? The apparent discomfort with this term justifies a little exploration into the definitions. Let us explore the definition of Biblical economics.

The reality is that there is no single definition of economics, and hence there is no single definition for biblical economics. As all learning is founded upon what we already know, so a definition for biblical economics must, too, be founded on what we already know. We can define the term by building upon what we already know of the terms respectively.

"Economics" is best known as a social science concerned chiefly with description and analysis of the production, distribution, and consumption of materials and services.

"Biblical" implies a relationship to the sacred scriptures of Christians comprising the Old Testament and the New Testament.

A simple combination of these terms would yield a definition like, A social science concerned chiefly with description and analysis of the production, distribution, and consumption of materials and services based upon the sacred scriptures of Christians comprising the Old Testament and the New Testament.

This definition is yet flawed because worldview economics begins with a limited view. It ignores the creative source of all the materials being produced. While the term *biblical* gives a clear indication of the paradigm, it does not make clear the essential element of conception within the economic function. Conception is the creative component that begins in the mind of God. It also is evident in the mind of the inventor or entrepreneur. The productive ideas and inventions are conceived long before they are ever produced or distributed. Therefore, biblical economics is the study of a Judeo-Christian paradigm for conception (creative power), production, and distribution of resources. It is simply God's system of reaping, sowing, living, and growing.

This definition is all-encompassing. It includes all that we do and all that we hope for. Economics not only relates to Wall Street and the Federal Reserve Bank, it's relevant to our daily lives. After all, satisfying our daily needs is an economic process. Even having a family dinner involves production, distribution, and consumption. In order to understand God's system, we are drawn to His owner's manual (the Holy Bible) for advice, counsel, discipline guidance, correction, and reproof. (2 Timothy 3:16)

Do you ever wonder what Bible verse demonstrates God's concern for economics? There are so many verses that do that, but the most patently evident is Deuteronomy 8:18: It tells us that God gives the power to obtain wealth in order to establish His covenant.

In this fundamental biblical economic verse we see that God has a good purpose for giving the power to obtain wealth. Obtaining wealth is clearly a matter relating to the conception, production, distribution of goods and services.

Patton's Paradigm

The next several sections discuss biblical paradigms and principles for economics. I hope that you will gain irrevocable insight into the relationship between faith, finances, the Word, and work.

A paradigm is a world view; it is the lens through which one sees the world around them. If you see the world from a Christian paradigm, you might likely recognize that we are in the world, but not of the world (John 17:14-15). You will likely see the world as the creation of a living God who is still involved in the lives of His creation.

I might go further to say that it is perhaps impossible to drive scholarly alignment without the acknowledgment that all human thought is value laden. Unless and until we all converge on a common set of values, divergent economic views will sing before the judges of truth and reason, and even antipathy. Some will last in contention why others will remain only in our history. The respectful thing to do is to declare and define our values, and dare to dialogue so that both sides may teach and learn.

In keeping with the premise that all learning is founded upon what is already known, it is appropriate to stake out a paradigm and endeavor to remain true to it. In respect to the perhaps extraordinary nature of this research, it claims a theological paradigm citing biblical and extra-biblical sources.

> Neo awakes after his traumatic rebirth out of the matrix and asks Morpheus, "Why do my eyes hurt?" Morpheus, answers softly, "They've never seen before."
>
> -The Matrix, a Warner Brothers Motion Picture

We must often choose our paradigm (or view of the world) with discernment and discrimination. The view from which we see the world determines truth, lies, reality, and the imagined for us. There is an overarching paradigm that anchors economic theory in the Word of God. Dr. Judd Patton summarizes this paradigm. Let's examine Patton's Biblical Economic Paradigm. Dr. Judd Patton is a Professor Emeritus of economics in Bellevue University in Nebraska, and a champion for Judeo-Christian thinking within government as well as all aspects of life.

God gives Christians three foundational building blocks for developing economic science.

God's Word is the foundation for all knowledge. Christian knowledge, understanding, and wisdom originate from fearing (respecting) God, by striving to keep His commandments, hating evil, and living by His every word (Eccles. 12:13; Prov. 8:13; Matt. 4:4). All other knowledge and wisdom is prophesied to come to nothing (1 Cor. 1:19–20).

1. Man is a purposeful being endowed with a spiritual essence, the spirit in man that gives him human mind and free will.
2. Man alone of God's creatures possesses the inner self of volition, self-awareness, the ability to choose goals and the means to fulfill them (1 Cor. 2:11). With the Holy Spirit, man has the capacity to build godly character in choosing right and resisting the wrong (2 Cor. 4:16; 10:4–5). Man acts; he values, prefers, and chooses (Prov. 15:22; 2 Cor. 9:7).
3. God, as Creator and Lawgiver (James 4:12; Isa. 33:22), has set in motion inexorable laws governing human behavior in whatever realm humans may interact—social, political, or economic.
4. These spiritual laws, when followed, generate and produce "life and prosperity" (Deut. 30:15–20; Exod. 20:3–17).
5. For individuals and societies to internalize these eternal principles is to cause a way of life that leads to harmony, peace, economic prosperity, and liberty (James 1:25).

Virtue bears spiritual and material fruit!

Many verses attest to this relationship between moral behavior and economic well-being.

- "And whatever he [the righteous] does shall prosper" (Ps. 1:3).
- "Blessed is the nation whose God is the LORD" (Ps. 33:12).
- "If they [the righteous] obey and serve Him, they shall spend their days in prosperity, and their years in pleasures" (Job 36:11).
- "This Book of the Law shall not depart from your mouth, but you shall meditate in it day and night, that you may observe to do according to all that is written in it. For then you will make your way prosperous, and then you will have good success" (Josh. 1:8).

From these three foundational building blocks a vital insight is discovered: the moral realm and the economic realm of production, consumption, and exchange are somehow interconnected. They are not hermetically sealed from one another as assumed by humanistic science (Patton, 1989).

Economics and the Family

That at that time ye were without Christ, being aliens from the commonwealth of Israel (Eph. 2:12, KJV).

The social and economic structure of the Roman-Greco world undoubtedly affected the lives of the first century Jews. Therefore, its effect on the hopes, dreams, and experiences of the progenitors of the Christian faith are inextricably linked to the New Testament. As the New Testament chronicles the formation of Christianity, it also depicts a unique and peculiar people on the brink of a radically new worldview.

In the first century the family—class, status, and patronage—framed the social structure of the Greco-Roman world. These factors determined the relationships among people and groups. Christians had a particularly beleaguered status, for they were a rejected sect from the Jews. Jews and their unique customs were tolerated, but Christians further threatened the status quo with their passionate appeals to the masses of poor. Rejected by the Jewish elite, Christian status was even another rung lower on the social-economic ladder.

As discussed earlier, the translation of the word *economics* is the "law of the house. House refers to household, which in essence means family. Generally, family and vocation determined class. The family was a rich social construct. It provided the vertical and horizontal axis of social location of an individual. One's ancestry determined class, status, and realizable carte blanche. If an individual was from the right family, he could strongly influence many aspects of Greco-Roman life.

Since most vocational training occurred in the context of families, a person's class was often established at birth. Farmers begot farmers, priests begot priests, traders begot traders, etc. The extended family or clan provided the circle of relations that gave breadth to influence or, in some cases, staffed armies. Marriage was for the purpose of producing legitimate offspring and more importantly to provide for the legal transfer of wealth via property.

The first century Greco-Roman society was dependent on agriculture. Every wealthy family owed their fortunes to agriculture. Wealth was acquired via inheritance, the spoils of war, extracted from debtors, or acquired from insolvent neighbors. The only exceptions to land-based wealth were merchants and customs collectors. Itinerant merchants would carry wines, spices, and exotic fruits, but essentially all other trading was local. Most of the Roman workforce was involved in farming, herding, and fishing. Hence, feast or famine hinged upon the harvest or the catch.

This land and food-based society is connected to Jesus's teaching in parables. He often analogized activities that were commonly understood in this largely farming community. Three of His first four recorded parables in Mark 4 elucidate the fundamentals of the sower and seeds. Although there were many vocations other than farming, most families had some association with agriculture. This is also evident is Jesus's admonishment to the scribes and Pharisees in Matthew 23:23. Even this elite group was accustomed to tendering herbs and spices from their first fruit.

Woe to you, scribes and Pharisees, hypocrites! For you tithe mint and dill and cumin, and have neglected the weightier provisions of the law.

Jesus, undoubtedly, was not referring to the inventory in their spice racks, but the agricultural commodities they possessed as a measure of productive commerce and net worth.

Reflections and Professions

1. Do you agree with Patton's Paradigm? Can you see more clearly through the biblical economic view?
2. Confess Deuteronomy 8:18 over your life and especially over your economic affairs. Profess this: "God gives (me) the power to obtain wealth in order to establish His covenant."
3. If your household is an economic system, what are the means of trade? What do you give? And what do you get in exchange?

2

Priest and Kings Forever

Although the whole earth is mine, you will be for
me a kingdom of priests and a holy nation.

—Exodus 19:6

To Be Priestly

Since we are called to be a kingdom of priests we must understand what it means to be a priest. It's surely instructive to imagine oneself as the icon image of the modern-day Catholic priest. When I Google the word *priest* I get images of a bald white guy with a black robe, white collar, and a cross. These images are followed by superheroes and villains. So what does is really mean to be a priest?

A priest is person sanctified for service to God and privileged to enter into His presence in the holy place, and to offer sacrifices. In the Christian priesthood, we are encouraged to enter into His presence with thanksgiving, and enter His throne room boldly. This privilege we are given is a direct result from our High Priest, Jesus, who has made the ultimate sacrifice for us all. We are to be living sacrifices, giving Him praise and devoting our lives to doing His will. In Old Testament times, the people of God dare not go to God. Only the ordained priest could do so. Biblical folklore suggests that the priest entered God's most Holy place with such fear and trepidation that the people would tie a rope to him just in case they needed to drag his body out. Jesus has sanctioned all believers and given us the privilege of going before the Lord.

> For we do not have a High Priest who cannot sympathize with our weaknesses, but was in all points tempted as we are, yet without sin. Let us therefore come boldly to the throne of grace, that we may obtain mercy and find grace to help in time of need. (Heb. 4:15–16)

Priests go before God to serve Him and intercede for others lacking the access. The believer is commanded to pray for others in the same way that Jesus did—that God's will be done in the earth as in heaven. Once we cross the threshold of spiritual adolescence and begin to pray for and serve others, we experience the goodness of God and His power working in us. We experience the priestly anointing whenever we go to the Lord on behalf of others. Whether praying for or otherwise ministering to our families, friends, or strangers in need, we are living out our call as priests. Christian men are often reminded that they are to be the priests in their homes. This command to be priestly is not for the men alone, for in Christ there is neither male nor female, Greek nor Jew, for we are all one in Christ Jesus.

> But you are a chosen people, a royal priesthood, a holy nation, a people belonging to God, that you may declare the praises of him who called you out of darkness into his wonderful light. (1 Pet. 2:9)

We are not only priests; we are royal priests. We have special rights as rulers and kings. Not as pompous potentates or exalted untouchables, but as vessels of honor, royalty, and servanthood to the people and their legacy. Priests are worshippers, ministers, and intercessors intimately acquainted with God. They carry Bibles.

To Be Royal

Our western cultural orientation diminishes our ability to fully comprehend the ways of royalty. An American Christian is more apt to know more about priests than kings. We a have superficial view of sovereignty because we live in a republic where people rule by representation. Conversely, in the Kingdom of God we are to represent our ruler wherever we find ourselves. While God's grace shines on a nation governed as a republic, there is a higher order of government that everyone is subject to. The Kingdom of God reigns on the just and unjust. We are citizens, subjects, and joint-heirs. We are in the world, but not of it. We need to become more in tune with the structure of the Kingdom of God if we are to appropriate its power. Kings are rulers, owners, landlords accountable for lands and people. They carry briefcases.

In a kingdom, the king dominates. There are no elections. Regency is a birthright. Kings are owners. They own land, property, and have responsibility for the lives of people. Kings have the responsibility to preserve the kingdom. The king must have a trans-generational view of the kingdom's wellbeing. Kings have vision, strategies, and plans. They have trusted advisors, captains, and those who serve the kingdom. Kings count the cost and enter into contracts and alliances. Kings take care of business.

The property of a business owner is like that of a king. He or she has private stewardship over the land and responsibility for the people who live on it, work within it, or otherwise benefit from its fruit. In the same way that we have co-regency in the Kingdom of God, business leaders and managers are co-regents over the affairs of an enterprise. The concept is familiar with the Western hierarchical structure. Leaders are served by the organization. Significance is greater at the top, and sacrifice at the bottom. While this model typifies Western culture, it is not the model given by Jesus.

> Just as the Son of Man did not come to be served, but to serve, and to give his life as a ransom for man. (Matthew 20:28)

God has given us the perfect model of Priest-King in Jesus. We see in Him the duality of sovereignty and sacrifice. The Priest-King is a servant-leader. We rarely find these qualities coexisting. There is, however, a powerfully synergistic and indivisible power of a Royal Priest. When you put together the knowledge of how to worship God and the knowledge of how to handle the means of production the result is a miraculous wealth transfer. That's when you put your Bible in your briefcase.

God has always wanted us to be priests and kings. The biblical record illustrates these qualities in some of its most honored subjects. The first king mentioned was Melchezidec, the priest-king (Gen. 14:18–20). He was so remarkable that he is known for receiving a tithe from Abraham, and bestowing blessing upon the father of Judeo-Christianity.

Moses was another noteworthy priest. Few might title Moses as a priest, but when we examine what he did versus any titles attributed to him, his royal priesthood is more evident. The prince of Egypt looks quite priestly standing between God and all of Israel. Moses was often in the position to pray to God to spare Israel from God's wrath. He interceded for Israel as well as for his sister Miriam when God wanted to punish her rebellion. Judging by Moses's actions, he is certifiably a priest.

Before we see Moses, the great deliverer, going before God on behalf of Israel, we see a prince and king in training. By the time of his departure from Egypt at age forty, Moses had learned all the knowledge needed to build and manage a kingdom. He had the equivalent of a PhD in every field of learning. He knew science, architecture, business, economics engineering, law, and astrology. Moses knew the ways of the world system, but there was a spiritual dimension that he was lacking.

The time would soon come when he would need to get in touch with his true self. A Levite by birth, Moses was full of the world's knowledge but ignorant of knowledge concerning the kingdom of God. Lacking a genuine self-love, Moses dramatized his own life paradox as he found himself in conflict between his spiritual heritage and a life of worldly assimilation. He lashed out in a dysfunctional rescue and killed an Egyptian for his cruelty to a Hebrew slave. Overwhelmed and perplexed by his rage of self-hate, he fled into the desert abandoning forever his life as an heir to the great Egypt.

> One day, after Moses had grown up, he went out to where his own people were and watched them at their hard labor. He saw an Egyptian beating a Hebrew, one of his own people. Glancing this way and that and seeing no one, he killed the Egyptian and hid him in the sand. (Exod. 2:11–12)

Moses's fate may seem peculiar. He was born a slave, raised as a prince, and destined to become a fugitive in the desert. Although we know the rest of the story, it is worth taking a moment to observe the significance of God's providence at work. God is always working to reestablish His divine order.

Reflections

1. Will you allow yourself to see yourself as royalty? What are your privileges as a child of the King?
2. Priests are intercessors who worship the Lord and stand between Him and the people. Are there people in your life who you feel responsible to pray for? It might be your family, friends, the people you work with, or perhaps a community or those you encounter in the course of doing your business. Reflect on who they are. Declare your priesthood to the Father by offering the following prayer.

Dear Jesus,

I accept Your commission as a royal priest. Please give me the sensitivity to pray for and with those in need, and the grace to pray earnestly to You; for You did not give me a spirit of fear, but of power and love and a sound mind. Help me to pray boldly, fervently, and continuously for the person who You bless me to meet and touch as I do my work unto You. Amen.

3

Contracting with God

Remember that God, your God gave you the strength
to produce all this wealth so as to confirm the covenant
that He promised your ancestors—as it is today.

Deuteronomy 8:18 (The Message)

It is comforting to know that God has given us the power to get wealth in order to accomplish His objective. His covenant will be confirmed. Since we know that He cannot fail, we can take confidence in the availability of wealth-getting power.

A covenant is, in simple terms, a contract. In this case it is a binding agreement with a God who can neither lie nor fail. God is prepared every day to uphold His part of the bargain. This is what He said to Abraham in Genesis 12:2–3:

I will make you into a great nation and I will bless you; I will make your name great, and you will be a blessing. I will bless those who bless you, and whoever curses you I will curse; and all peoples on earth will be blessed through you.

As God spoke these words, He set into motion the Jews, Jesus, and the Christian faith for all eternity. Some have received and appropriated this promise for centuries, while others of us are just beginning to unlock the secrets of this awesome promise.

To gain insight on the social economic factors surrounding the formation of Old Testament scripture, it is important to examine the covenants of God. His covenants provide the entitlements and boundaries for Israel's belief systems and its physical survival. Biblical covenants are different from the contemporary English understanding of covenant. A covenant is generally thought to be formal, binding mutual agreement between parties. A look at what's referred to as the Adamic Covenant (Gen. 2:16–17) illustrates a more unilateral construction of the agreement.

The LORD God commanded the man, saying, "From any tree of the garden you may eat freely; but from the tree of the knowledge of good and evil you shall not eat, for in the day that you eat from it you will surely die."

God's impending sanctions don't seem in the least bit mutual nor do they seem much at all like a contract, agreement or promise. The deal here is simple, if you do it, you will die. What, then, is the proper context and definition of the term *covenant*?

The Hebrew word for covenant is *berith*. Attempts to derive the meaning of the term from etymology have not led to precise conclusions. Many scholars, however, link its meaning to an Assyrian word, which means "to bind or fetter." Additionally, the form of such agreements or treaties follows that of the suzerainty treaties of Hittite kings. Suzerainty treaties were drawn up unilaterally by the conquering monarch of the captured vassal. The vassal was obliged to pledge allegiance in exchange for the help and protection of the suzerain. While covenants between humans are bilaterally negotiated, covenants with God are like suzerain covenants. The covenant forms the arrangements unilaterally originated from the superior party. It was customary in this region and time to be party to such one-sided arrangements.

God is sovereign. In other words, God's laws are nonnegotiable, so it's a capital idea to understand them. Being born in a democratic republic sometimes handicaps us from grasping the norms of a kingdom. We will discuss later how breaking an economic law also breaks a covenant law.

What are the terms of your agreement with the Creator and owner of the universe?

Wealth Transfer Contract

> The LORD said to Abram after Lot had parted from him, "Lift up your eyes from where you are and look north and south, east and west. All the land that you see I will give to you and your offspring forever. I will make your offspring like the dust of the earth, so that if anyone could count the dust, then your offspring could be counted." (Gen. 13:14– 16)

Abram was given the wealth transfer covenant. It promised that he would have (1) all the land as far as he could see, and (2) that his people would be a numerous as the dust of the earth. These are the two essential ingredients to wealth—land and people.

Being a child of God does not require you to take an oath of poverty. Perhaps you only need to be reminded that there is a better way to think and a better way to act in order to activate the Kingdom wealth transfer into your life. Now, before you relegate this message to another prosperity gospel rant, recall that the reason for wealth is for the establishment of God's covenant.

In one hand we have our briefcases and in the other our Bibles. We have the knowledge and the power to appropriate God's wealth covenant in a way that honors Him and works for the sake of His Kingdom. We enter into business often to make a living or to acquire respect and status, but we, at some point in our walk as believers, begin to wonder how our work matters. How can we bless the Kingdom by selling widgets, boxes, or preparing tax returns? Is accepting less wealth somehow more Christian? Is doing my job with integrity, ethics, and compassion for others sufficient to fulfill my responsibility as Christian in the marketplace?

As children of the God of abundance, it follows that we should be positive producers in the earth. Perhaps there is even an expectation that we be good stewards and make the most of what God has given us. There is a fundamental economic principle at play that determines our productivity and prosperity—it is the principle of sowing and reaping. It matters what you sow, and it matters where you sow. Jacob's life gives a poignant example of this principle.

Jacob was a good-hearted economist. He, like most of us, was a self-interested, calculating optimizer. We are designed by God to self-preserve life and to use our intellect to get what we want and need. He was a man who knew what he wanted and was confident to use all his gifts, talents and faculties to get it. After conning his brother for his birthright, he left home to seek love and good fortune. Led away by his own desire, he found himself working for an even cleverer conman named Laban. He worked seven years in order to marry Laban's daughter Rachel, the apple of Jacob's eye, only to be subject to the famous bait and switch. Laban substituted his older daughter, Leah, in the wedding chamber and congratulated Jacob on his new marriage. In a show of chivalry and unrequited love, Jacob agreed to work another seven years to wed Rachel, the woman of his dreams. More importantly, he worked dutifully and tithed faithfully, and yet he did not prosper.

Why didn't he prosper? A tithing child of God with a birthright should always prosper, right? Jacob did not begin to prosper until he got his own land. He was not a lord of any land. He was being lorded. Laban, the lord of the land, was being blessed to prosper. He even begged Jacob not to go. Laban confessed to Jacob:

> And Laban said unto him, I pray thee, if I have found favour
> in thine eyes, tarry: for I have learned by experience that the
> LORD hath blessed me for thy sake. (Gen. 30:27)

Laban, a more astute conman, knew all along that Jacob was his golden goose. It was not until Jacob had this epiphany that he began to appropriate the wealth covenant for himself. He finally professed to Laban.

> For it was little which thou hadst before I came, and it is now increased unto a multitude; and the LORD hath blessed thee since my coming: and now when shall I provide for mine own house also? (Gen. 30:29)

Then Jacob negotiated a deal with Laban where he would have his own land and flock. Jacob was shrewder this time to leave a lot of value on the table to convince Laban that he was getting the better deal. Jacob took the lesser land and the spotted sheep, but his flocks multiplied many times over. He had finally appropriated the wealth covenant.

In the same way, your employers are benefitting from your faithful tithe. God may be blessing your house, but it is not a place of enterprise. If God is going to pour out a blessing, you must give Him some place to pour. God said,

> Bring ye all the tithes into the storehouse, that there may be meat in mine house, and prove me now herewith, saith the LORD of hosts, if I will not open you the windows of heaven, and pour you out a blessing, that there shall not be room enough to receive it. (Mal. 3:10)

He intends to pour a blessing that you won't have room enough to receive it. You need to have a room to begin with. If it is not your room, then where can He pour? God says, "I will bless the land you possess." If you are not the possessor, then your tithing is benefitting those whom you work for. You need to own something—a lot, a pot, or something.

> And Abram said, LORD God, what wilt thou give me, seeing I go childless, and the steward of my house is this Eliezer of Damascus? And Abram said, Behold, to me thou hast given no seed: and, lo, one born in my house is mine heir. And, behold, the word of the LORD came unto him, saying, This shall not be thine heir; but he that shall come

forth out of thine own bowels shall be thine heir. (Gen.
15:2–4)

We know Abraham as the father of our faith, but it wasn't until
he was old that God blessed him with a child. Even though God had
promised fatherless Abram that he would be the father of many nations.
Abraham asked, "God, how am I going to be a great father with lots
of kids when I have no seed?" (Gen. 15:3). Abraham was not trying
to grow apples or pomegranates. He said he had no seed. That's not
a good thing if your vision is to be the father of many nations. His
wife affirmed his deficiency when she laughed, and said, "Will I yet
have pleasure, my husband being old, too?" What God gave him was
better than any drug on the market today. The Holy Spirit restored his
vitality. God gave Abram the seed he needed so that he could sow into
Christian destiny.

Although Abram was invigorated and filled with promise, he and
Sarai were yet unable to conceive. So they decided to take matters in
their own hands. Sarai offered her servant Hagar as a surrogate to bear
Abram's child. Abram jumped on the opportunity and was given a son,
Ishmael. This was not the son of promise, but the son a fleshly self-
reliance. God was not done yet. He arranged a seemingly impossible
situation to show the immutability of His promise to Abraham. Not
long thereafter, Sarai, in her revived body, birthed Isaac through whom
would come the nation of Israel. God's promise was fulfilled and
kingdoms were birthed through the unlikeliest vessels. God seems to
favor underdogs, misfits, and second-chancers.

God's gifts come without repentance (Rom. 11:29). Whatever He
gives you, you've got forever. You may use it, or abuse it, but you still
have it.

Years later Abraham still had promise inside him. After God restored
his reproductive prowess, Abraham stayed vigorous. So, after his wife
Sarai died, Abraham got married again and started another family. He
married Kethura who gave him four sons, one of whom is Midian, the
father of the Midianites. His settlement beneath Mount Sinai would be
the backdrop for Moses's unique encounter with the Most High God.

Now we return to Moses in the desert on the run with a briefcase
full of PhDs. Moses meets a fearfully made woman at the well. She is
beautiful and strong. Moses defends her and she takes him to meet her

father, Jethro, the priest of Midian. Jethro is a priest, who knows how to sacrifice and worship the Lord. He's got one problem…well, really he's got seven problems: seven beautiful daughters and no sons. Although his daughters naturally have no seed, they are incubators of the holy priesthood in God's covenant. These girls know more about the things of the spirit than Moses has ever heard. So Moses marries Zipporah and Jethro takes a burnt offering. This consummation restores the Priest-King covenant and the wealth transfer. This occurs just as Israel is being prepared for her great exodus from the bondage of Egypt. In one family is the knowledge of the priesthood and the know-how to handle wealth. This reunion consummates the royal priesthood of God's peculiar people, royal priesthood, and holy nation.

Reflections

1. Have you read and remembered the promises of Gods contract with you?
2. Are you regularly looking for them to manifest in your life?
3. What relationships or agreements are you in that may be robbing you of your promised blessing?
4. Are you giving God enough vessels to pour into—like a business, and investment or other appreciating assets
5. Where are you sowing? Are you sowing in your field or in someone else's? Are you possessing the lands or the vessels for the Lord to pour into your life?
6. Many of us are working hard for someone else's benefit and blessings. Who are the Labans in your life?

Dear Lord,

I am so grateful for the promises you have made to me. Forgive me for striving on my own. You are such a good father. You have been careful to provide for me, and I have been careless or overlook what you have already provided. Please grant me wisdom to possess the land and place the pots for you to pour into. Help me to see and separate from the relationships that our robbing me of my portion of your promised blessing.

4

Economic Commandments and Principles

The earth is the Lord's and everything in it, the world, and all who live in it; for he founded it upon the seas and established it upon the waters.

—Psalm 24:1–2

The Ten Commandments are universal truths in lock step with economic laws. They are broadly known and accepted. Even those who mistakenly write off the Old Testament as no longer valid under the New Testament's dispensation of grace never argue against the validity of the Ten Commandments. Even those societies that mistakenly deny the sovereignty of God, still endorse God's prohibitions against killing, stealing, and lying. In other words, even when they don't accept the first table of commandments, which addresses how to successfully relate to God, they still accept the second table, which addresses how to successfully relate to other persons. Even agnostics, atheists Hindus, Buddhists, Taoists, and scientologists, who reject the first table, elect to live by some derivation of the second table.

Economic debate has always centered on the overarching theme of ownership. Whether observing scholarly grudge matches between capitalists and socialists, or kingdom-paradigm-land-possessors and liberation theology protesters, the questions are, "Whose is it?" and "Who has rights of access and control?" Ownership is the most basic of economic issues.

- In the sixth commandment, murder is prohibited. This is not simply because murder is a bad thing to do. It relates back to the economic issue of ownership. It is because none of us can lay claim to life-creating power. The underlying message is, "Don't take what does not belong to you."
- The seventh commandment, "Thou shall not commit adultery," while not minimizing the paramount importance of marriage and family, it is a standard of covenant keeping. Will a man who cheats on his wife cheat on a contract? You decide.
- The eighth commandment, "You shall not steal," recognizes that private stewardship has been assigned to someone. To wrongly take property of another against his will is a violation of our covenant with God. Without this basic respect, and the requisite reinforcement of property rights, the entire economic system unravels. Incentive to work is corrupted, production of value is halted, and scarcity prevails.
- The ninth commandment, "Don't bear false witness," is the standard of integrity that is essential to any agreement.

Misrepresentations of the truth lead to stealing and covenant breaking.

- Finally, the tenth commandment, "Don't covet," wraps all the others up into a reminder of God's abundant Lordship. It is as if He is saying, "I have given you everything you need to be fruitful and to multiply, so don't look upon another desiring what he has. Be the fearfully and wonderfully made child of God that I made you. Looking upon your neighbor's possessions with a burning desire will lead you to kill, steal, or lie. So, don't even think that way.

Our Creator has established laws that govern our relationship with Him and with each other. He has given us wealth-producing power and an unquenchable desire to sustain life and value via the cycle of economic conception, production, distribution, and consumption.

Biblical Economic Principles

Principles are foundational truths that undergird a system of beliefs. Believing that the Bible is a guide to economics is necessary but not sufficient to apply these truths to one's daily reaping and sowing. The ten principles that follow intend to provide a framework for acting in the biblical economic way. (See Appendix- Biblical Economic Principles Summary)

1. Trust the Source

Genesis declares God as the source of the earth and all creation. The fact the He placed the reproductive capability in everything created is a testimony of His divine plan for the production, distribution, and consumption of resources "Have no other God before me (God)" is the primary economic commandment. To have no other God but God means to trust in Him for our source of guidance, judgment, and especially provision.

Secular economics, by definition and practice, ignores the source of the world's economic matter. An often-accepted definition of economics is that of British economist, Lionel Robbins: "Economics is the study of the use of scarce resources which have alternative uses."

Another well-know economist, Thomas Sowell goes on to say,

The Garden of Eden was a system for the production of and distribution of goods and services, but it was not an economy because everything was available in unlimited abundance. Without scarcity there is no need to economize and therefore no economics. (Sowell, 2000)

This doctrine misses the patent demonstration of the inextricable link between God's way and the distribution of provision for life. While living in a place named "Pleasure," the only scarcity in the Garden was the forbidden fruit. It was limited to zero access. When Adam chose scarcity over God's abundance, it cost him. It cost all of humanity. The first family's cost of food escalated by the additional toil to cultivate the now-cursed ground. They were summarily evicted from Eden to a less pleasurable habitat. Their economics were very much affected by their choice to disobey God's guidance.

Cursed is the ground because of you; through painful toil you will eat of it all the days of your life. It will produce thorns and thistles for you and you will eat the plants of the field. By the sweat of your brow you will eat your food until you return to the ground, since from it you were taken…So the LORD God banished him from the Garden of Eden to work the ground from which he had been taken. (Gen. 3:17–19, 23)

God set in motion the dominion of humankind and the ecological food chain. There is nothing in the earth that did not originate from that which He created. God's sovereignty must not be taken for granted in the study of economic matter. Jesus reinforces this principle when He declares, "You cannot serve God and mammon [material wealth]" (Luke 16:13). The divine order established in the genesis must also be the goal of economic order. Adam was placed there to cultivate and replenish. Most importantly, he was with God. Therefore, the purpose of the economic order is to provide a standard of living that not only meets people's basic physical needs (such as food, clothing, shelter) but also facilitates their pursuit of higher values, including the highest value of all, the union with God.

2. Manage Wisely

Biblical Principle number one is trust the source. Number two flows directly from it. While seeing God as the source, we have a responsibility to manage what He has entrusted us with. Whether the resources are plants and herbs, household finances, dollars and cents or corporate assets, the source and the responsibilities are the same. Biblical Economic Principle 2 is Manage Wisely.

For what purpose did God put Adam in the garden? Genesis 2:15 says, He put him in the garden to "dress and to keep it." Some translations say to "cultivate it." As Adam's offspring, we are required to carry out this command. God commanded Adam, the first family, to be fruitful and replenish. The earth is abundant, yet abuses will result in imbalances, extinction, poverty, and even death.

We must not disrupt the created order in the course of cultivating and replenishing the earth. The Bible declares the earth is the Lord's (Prov. 24:1). It also says in Leviticus 25:23, "The land shall not be sold in perpetuity, for the land is Mine." He gave us the responsibility to manage the earth and He expects us to continue cultivating to produce fruit for His Kingdom.

It might not seem readily apparent, yet everything we have comes from the earth. It comes from the land or the sea. Even the dollars we spend were once part of a tree. We have a responsibility to manage wisely what He has given us. Another term for management is stewardship. As stewards we are the managers of the earth and everything in it. Whether referring to land, sea, forest, trees, dollars, or gifts and talents, we must be good stewards of hat which the Source has provided.

What garden has He placed you in—a factory, office, boardroom, or industry? Are you using every opportunity to cultivate and replenish? The best way that we, as believers, can replenish our gardens is by inviting the Lord into it, and then asking Him for the grace and favor to cultivate it for His glory today.

3. Do What You Do Best

This above all: to thine own self be true, and it must follow, as the night the day, Thou canst not then be false to any man. (Shakespeare's *Hamlet*)

Each individual is called to reflect God's creative nature through the application of human capital (ingenuity, labor) to creation. Mankind was given the divine mandate to be fruitful, multiply and subdue the earth (Gen. 1:28). We were purposed to be cultivators of the rich earth. Genesis 2:15 speaks specifically of the purpose of mankind. It states, "Then the LORD God took the man and put him into the Garden of Eden to cultivate it and keep it" (NASB).

We are creative beings made in the image of God. We are wonderfully and fearfully fashioned with unique gifts and talents that, when combined with God's provision of creation, produce value. Humans are sometimes defined as "toolmakers" (*homo faber*). This recognizes our creativity as we take what we are given and work it into something new (Tiemstra, 1998). In godly wisdom we find knowledge of witty inventions (Prov. 8:12). Work must enable the expression of our God-given talent to create. Each individual is equipped to share his or her creativity through their vocation (Gronbacher, 1998).

We are not blessed alike, but uniquely and exceptionally fashioned and called into the earth to fulfill a divinely assigned purpose. God has crafted each person with a unique constitution, certain talents and proclivities, and finally a personal identity. But to each one of us grace has been given as Christ apportioned it. This is why Scripture says, "When he ascended on high, he led captive a host of captives and gave gifts to men" (Eph. 4:7–8). Use the gifts He gave you. Do your thing. Stay in your lane. These are all ways of saying, "Do what you do best." Then we all will be the more blessed.

As the psalmist said, "For you created my inmost being; you knit me together in my mother's womb. I praise you because I am fearfully and wonderfully made; your works are wonderful, I know that full well" (Ps. 139:13–14).

4. Be Responsible!

As every man hath received the gift, even so minister the
same one to another, as good stewards of the manifold grace
of God. (1 Pet. 4:10)

Each individual person (or enterprise) is given the opportunity for
stewardship and the accountability for the disposition of resources. This
is a God-given inalienable right. God gives each person a measure of
personal resources such as labor and ingenuity. This principle is clearly
illustrated in the parable of the talents (Matt. 25). We find no example
of communal ownership in the Old Testament apart from the family
(Tiemstra, 1990). God brings us in as individuals, we establish accounts
of stewardship as individuals, and we depart earth's time and space
continuum as individuals. We share our gifts and talents with others in
order to produce value, yet we are not ever absolved from our individual
responsibility before God.

The two New Testament stories that are often cited as support for
a communal dispensation is the story of Ananias and Sapphira and the
"all things in common" verses in Acts 4:32–35. Even though there was
sharing, which God expects us to do, it was not mandated to the degree
that individual decisions of stewardship were subsumed to that of the
community. Ananias and Sapphira lied to Peter about how much of the
proceeds of their land sale they donated to the church. This couple's
exemplary execution was the result of their misrepresentations, not their
failure to surrender all their possessions.

"Didn't it belong to you before it was sold? And after it was sold,
wasn't the money at your disposal? Why have you conceived this deed
in your heart?" (Acts 5:4).

A subtle message of this biblical lesson is the expectation of discretion
coupled with integrity. The parable of the talents also illustrates the
accountability for one's disposition of resources. Peter maintained
that the choice of disposition of the assets belongs to the household.
God's divine order for the family and the stewardship of their resources
requires individual stewardship and accountability.

Be responsible or "response-able." Be able to respond when the
Master calls you to account for how you have stewarded what He has

given you. Your gifts, talents, job, ministry are assets for which He expects a return. How is your account?

Be responsible. "You have been faithful of little, so I will make you master over much" (Matt. 5:21).

5. Sow and Reap!

Remember this, whoever sows sparingly will also reap sparingly, and whoever, sows bountifully will also reap bountifully. (1 Cor. 9:6)

Each individual is given the right and obligation to work and productively share in God's provision for their basic needs of food, clothing, and shelter. Work is of God.

Adam was placed in the garden for the purpose of cultivating it. There was ample food in the rich foliage of Eden. In the wilderness there was provision of manna and water. This quintessential provision of God is articulated again in Matthew 6:25–33.

"But seek first his kingdom and his righteousness, and all these things will be given to you as well" (Matt. 6:33).

God has provided food and clothing for every creature in the kingdom of God. Adam's dominion over all the creatures provided clothing for him after the fall. Shelter was not spoken of until Noah's construction of the ark. Yet, we see in the story of Noah God providing shelter before the need arose. It had not yet rained, but Noah would have shelter by heeding God's voice and applying his ingenuity and labor to the materials in the earth (gopher wood and pitch). God always makes provision ahead of the need. It is always already there. It requires work to appropriate his provision. This is made evident in the creation passage. The creation sequence starts at bottom of the food chain and progress up to humans. He made humans only after everything they would ever need was already in Eden.

Humans, unlike the birds fed of the Father in Matthew 6:26, have an obligation to work. As the author of Ecclesiastes put it, "There is nothing better for a man than to eat and drink and tell him that his labor is good. This also I have seen, that it is from the hand of God" (Eccles. 2:24).

The writer of Psalm 104 regards man's work as natural as the lion's instinct to hunt. The lions roar for their prey and seek their food from God. The sun rises, and they steal away; they return and lie down in their dens. Then man goes out to his work, to his labor until evening. (Ps. 104:21–23)

Paul virtually established a law of social economics in his announcement in 2 Thessalonians 3:10.

For even when we were with you, we gave you this rule: "If a man will not work, he shall not eat." We hear that some among you are idle. They are not busy; they are busybodies. Such people we command and urge in the Lord Jesus Christ to settle down and earn the bread they eat.

On the other side, the principle proclaimed by our Lord remains the basis of society: the worker deserves his wages (Luke 10:7).

Sow your labor and ingenuity and reap a harvest! Reaping and sowing is more than what you put in the offering plate. It is how you lay your life down every day to produce value for the Kingdom of God.

6. Collaborate

*Now he that plants and he that waters are one: and every man
shall receive his own reward according to his own labor. For we
are God's fellow workers: you are God's field. (1 Cor. 3:8–9)*

Social cooperation in the form of work is essential to prosperous
stewardship. Work is to prosperity and proper stewardship as sex is to
reproduction and populating earth. It is an unquenchable God-given
drive within us to ensure the production of resources from creation,
and the interaction among individuals that leads to unity. Humans
are social by nature. Self-sufficiency is a neoclassical myth. Prosperity
is only possible through productive interaction with others and the
division of labor (work).

One person's need is another's surplus. In the Bible as early as Cain
and Abel, we see God gifting one brother as a farmer and the other as
a herdsman. Neither being exclusively vegetarian nor carnivore, but
both contributed his gift to balance family feasts. Since we are endowed
differently, there is relative scarcity. We are not blessed equally, but
equitably according to our own particular portions of divine enabling,
provisional grace. There are differences in talents and differences
in proximity to resources that affords better access to the means of
production. It is the existence of such differences that draws us together,
and demands our interaction, and mutually satisfying transaction for
talents, ideas, and resources.

"From him [Christ] the whole body, joined and held together by
every supporting ligament, grows and builds itself up in love, as each
part does its work" (Eph. 7:21).

We must work together. It's amazing how far our culture has gone
with the notion of zero-sum game competition. When in fact the word,
competition, literally means "to strive together." It is derived from the
Latin *com,* which means "together," and *petere*, meaning "to strive or
petition." In other words, we strive together (not against) to achieve our
individual and collective best.

There is a considerable trend toward blurred lines across; religious
and secular, church and state, and business and ministry. The walls have

come down. Yet, some are bound by the limitations of the past. There is beauty in diversity and power in cooperation. Reach out and grab a hand today and say, "Let's do something great together," and make our Father smile.

7. Respect Ownership

You shall not move your neighbor's landmark. (Deut. 19:14)

Private property stewardship is essential to economic freedom, which is an essential element of human freedom. Even though our biblical economic principles fully acknowledge God's ownership of the earth and everything in it, they nevertheless recognize that individuals must have private, independent stewardship rights to land and property. Human freedom involves the right to life, liberty, and the pursuit of happiness in a context that is free from sin and governmental tyranny. Economic freedom is simply the right to sufficiency or unencumbered access to God's provision. Slavery is the extreme deprivation of freedom. The slave is not only stripped of property but also is further reduced to exist as the property of another. Similarly, when an individual is deprived of the right to exercise stewardship and made wholly dependent upon others, the individual is as a slave. He is forcibly made beholden to another for basic provisions and the means of production.

Private property stewardship affords the primary resource to combine one's labor and ingenuity into valuable produce. Without property rights individuals are as slaves, lessees, or borrowers. Proverbs 22:7 says, "The borrower is slave to the lender."

Gregory Gronbacher says it best in the following quote: "Human nature requires private ownership for the successful navigation of the material world, for the care of family members and the weak, and the acquisition of virtue through generosity and good stewardship. The corresponding duties that accompany this right include the call to generosity, the requirement of good stewardship, and the vocation of productivity and creativity" (Gronbacher, 2002).

The economic atrophy experienced under Zimbabwe's President Mugabe is a classic illustration of the result of disrespecting property rights. He gave large payments to rioting veterans and the promise of land that would be seized from commercial owners without compensation. He encouraged invasions and the pegging out of claims on properties. As landowners and their workers were attacked and beaten, commercial investments halted, farmland went fallow, employment nose-dived, and food prices soared due to shortages ("Special Report on Zimbabwe," 2002).

Respect for private ownership is foundational to a prosperous economy. Consistent with the well-founded principle that we reap what we sow, we must respect private ownership so our ownership is respected. While respecting land rights might be a no-brainer, we sometimes weaken this bedrock by perpetuating the popular norm of unauthorized duplicating media such as music and videos. As believers in business it behooves us to understand copyrights, patents, and trademarks. Is your property safe while your neighbor is being pilfered?

"For every breach of trust whether it is for ox, for donkey, for sheep, or clothing or any lost thing… both parties will come before the judges" (Exod. 22:9).

8. Give Opportunity

Then the master called the servant in. "You wicked servant,"
he said, "I canceled all that debt of yours because you
begged me to. Shouldn't you have had mercy on your fellow
servant just as I had on you?" (Matt. 18:32–33).

Economic efforts of one must not deprive others of their rights as stewards and the right to work (Tiemstra, 1990). This biblical principle is attached to the prohibition of usury upon the poor, and the proper treatment of hired servants.

Do not charge your brother interest, whether on money or food
or anything else that may earn interest. (Deut. 23:19)

The charging of interest upon the needy, in effect, makes the lender to benefit from the hardship of another. The enslaved borrower having to surrender wealth in order to provide for the family is less than a show of love for thy neighbor, and was thought to be unjust. Land upon which to work was the first defense against poverty. Those without land were provided work until they could redeem their land by purchase or in the year of Jubilee. Provisions were made for the gleaning of fields to insure the basic family needs were met. Other provisions relating to just balances and the prohibition of bribes and other contortions of justice were instituted to mitigate the advantage to the rich over the poor.

In a business activity interest is appropriate as exchange of benefits. The borrower pays for the right to have resources earlier than otherwise available. The lender is sowing seed in expectation of a harvest from the enterprise of the borrower. Interest in this sense is not expressly prohibited in the Bible. It is even encouraged by Jesus in the parables of the talents and pounds.

On the other hand, excessive interest was consistently disdained. For if a farmer borrows grain for seedtime and experiences crop failure, his or her lands may be in jeopardy of repossession. Although the standard of commerce is that the parties be made whole, it is not God's will that the borrower lose permanent access to the means of production. The Bible affords rules of redemption and the recurring grace at the time of Jubilee. The Old Testament provides for the forgiving of all debts every seven years. Under the grace of the New Covenant, our efforts must not contribute to disabling another from working and providing for his or her family. Exorbitant interest rates, which are generally charged to those least able to pay, and collateral requirements that induce property seizure deprive God's people of stewardship and reduce them to indentured servants.

"He that by usury [exorbitant interest, Strong 5392] and unjust gain increaseth his substance, he shall gather it for him that will pity the poor" (Prov. 28:8, KJV).

We must respect the individual's right to work and earn rewards. We see abuses in this area in China and other developing economies where workers are required to work off debts. Wages are sometimes held back for fees or penalties relating to work performance. The result is an insufficient wage, an unpayable debt, and deprivation of the worker's God-given economic freedom.

Karol Wojtyla (Pope John Paul II) explains it this way: "A person who is deprived of something he can call 'his own,' and of the possibility of earning a living through his own initiative, comes to depend on the social machine and on those who control it. This makes it much more difficult for him to recognize his dignity as a person, and hinders progress towards the building up of an authentic human community" (John Paul II, 1991).

Give opportunity by paying a fare wage and releasing debts whenever possible. Be sensitive to your workers and your suppliers' burdens so that you, in the name of doing business, don't become the final the blow to their demise. Give second chances, opportunities to recover, and opportunities to earn your business and your trust. We have all been new employees, start-ups, and debtors.

So give opportunity!

9. Give to the Poor

But just as you excel in everything—in faith, in speech, in knowledge, in complete earnestness and in your love for us—see that you also excel in this grace of giving. (2 Cor. 8:7)

Stewardship includes the responsibility to produce sufficient provision for the marginalized and the poor. Beneficence is virtue written in the Old Testament Law and reinforced by Jesus's teachings. There are many provisions in the Law, such as canceling debts, freeing slaves, and redeeming land that are designed to remedy poverty. God declared the negligence to caring for widows and orphans a sin punishable by death (Exod. 22:22–24). Jesus says in Matthew 26:6, "The poor you will always have with you, but you will not always have me." He complemented the Old Testament in several instances where he draws attention to the cry of the poor and our responsibility to care for them within the commonwealth of the Kingdom of God. The stories about the rich young ruler (Matt. 19:16–22), and the rich man and Lazarus (Luke 16:19–31) illustrate our responsibility for the poor. Giving to the poor is demonstration of our Christ-likeness. Paul implores our giving as a test of our sincere love.

But just as you excel in everything—in faith, in speech, in knowledge, in complete earnestness and in your love for us—see that you also excel in this grace of giving. I am not commanding you, but I want to test the sincerity of your love by comparing it with the earnestness of others. For you know the grace of our Lord Jesus Christ, that though he was rich, yet for your sakes he became poor, so that you through his poverty might become rich.

(2 Cor. 8:7–9)

As wise stewards, believers in business must never confuse business with charity. As Jesus said, "Behold, I send you forth as sheep in the midst of wolves: be ye therefore wise as serpents, and harmless as doves" (Matt. 10:16). The more you manage wisely or shrewdly, the more that can be charitably given. In the same way that we strategically plan to make profits, we can also strategically plan to give to charitable endeavors.

Since 1972 there have been ninety-five studies examining the link between social performance and financial performance. Most recently, a New University study concludes that charitable contributions by U.S. companies do enhance future revenue growth. Giving is good for your business. When it comes to business, Bill Gates and Warren Buffett are superb givers to emulate. They together launched the Giving Pledge in 2010. It asks the commitment of the world's most wealthy to dedicate the majority of their wealth to philanthropy. They each led the way by pledging billions and many others followed.

10. Respect the Law of the Land

Everyone must submit himself to the governing authorities, for there is no authority except that which God has established. The authorities that exist have been established by God. (Rom. 13:1)

Government's role is to protect the rights of private ownership and to provide the balance of justice between work and wealth. Government's role is to enforce laws, contracts, and set standards in a way that achieves a reliable context for economic activity to flourish. Its role should be that of a protector of wealth and much less a distributor. Private property ought to be protected by government and from government. Without such protection from theft, deceit, and murder, economic chaos will prevail. So we ought to appreciate the law of the land, as it provides the context for prosperity in business.

The Old Testament had strict legislation against moving landmarks and stealing livestock. God warns Israel upon their insistence on having a king that there was a cost to pay. His desire was that Israel remain a people under His dominion. Yet, they insisted on having a king like other nations. So God delegated authority to governors. Kingdoms and governments have dominion and sovereignty only under God.

Government's role as a standard setter is illustrated in the Biblical example of establishing weights and standards. God commanded justice in exchange of goods and services.

"The LORD abhors dishonest scales, but accurate weights are his delight" (Prov. 11:10).

It is government's role to protect the individual worker's rights, but not at the expense of the enterprise's rights. The fulcrum of justice can only establish this balance between work and wealth. Barring feudalistic means of acquiring property the owners of capital will have a profound advantage over the workers. These powers in the hands of sinful humans will naturally result in some injustices if not checked by the government. So governments establish base employment laws to ensure workers are paid for work and not abused. This agency is consistent with biblical laws.

> Do not take advantage of a hired man who is poor and needy, whether he is a brother Israelite or an alien living in

one of your towns. Pay him his wages each day before sunset, because he is poor and is counting on it. Otherwise he may cry to the LORD against you, and you will be guilty of sin.

(Deut. 24:14–15)

The limits of government's intervention have not yet been clearly and practically articulated. The US Declaration of Independence and Constitution represent the most carefully constructed guidelines for the limits of government. Yet the carrying out of these axioms has been fraught with misinterpretations and abuses. The discovery of the optimal measure of individual liberty and governmental protections would be a profound contribution to the field of Christian Economics. Pope John Paul proposes a useful description of such principle.

"There is certainly a legitimate sphere of autonomy in economic life which the State should not enter. The State, however, has the task of determining the juridical framework within which economic affairs are to be conducted, and thus of safeguarding the prerequisites of a free economy, which presumes a certain equality between the parties, such that one party would not be so powerful as practically to reduce the other to subservience" (John Paul II, 1991).

Reflections and Professions

1. Think of your job, business, or career as the garden that God has placed you in. As you prepare to go to work, profess to yourself: "God put me in this (job, business, or assignment) to cultivate and replenish it."
2. What are your unique passions and gifting? What would you do if you did not need to earn money for a living? What are the things that you do that put you in the zone where it does not even feel like work?
3. How is your account? Are you giving God a return on the gifts and talents that He has given you? What has He given you that could be better cultivated?
4. How are you sowing your life in a way that produces value for the Kingdom of God?
5. Who can you collaborate with? Take the first today to combine you efforts with another.
6. Since you understand the principle "you reap what you sow," is there someone who owes you a debt? What would happen if you released them? Is there someone to whom you can give a second chance? Do it!
7. Take a little extra money with you then next time you go out. Then look for an opportunity to give it away. How about that person begging on the street? Don't walk by them today but buy them a coffee or cold drink. Or pay for the coffee or lunch for the person behind you. Ask the cashier to tell them, "You have a Father in Heaven who loves you. He wants you to know that today." Leave the scene before they can thank you or even know that you were the instrument of their blessing.

5

Doing the King's Business

Whatever you do, work at it with all your heart, as working for the Lord, not for men, since you know that you will receive an inheritance from the Lord as a reward. It is the Lord Christ you are serving. *Colossians 3:23*

As we walk out our destinies as Believers in Business (BIB), our minds are in a process of ongoing renewal. We are changing from the view of godly persons going to work to the paradigm of one going to work for God. The BIB knows that s/he works for King and not for men. Remember, we are ambassadors. Those who accept this call are really marketplace ministers disguised as doctors, lawyers, butchers, bakers, engineers, managers, and teachers.

> And He has committed to us the message of reconciliation. We are therefore Christ's ambassadors, as though God were making his appeal through us. We implore you on Christ's behalf: Be reconciled to God. (2 Cor. 5:19–20)

Let us be reminded that we work for the King. The King deserves our best. So we must not be deterred by the people we encounter along the way. People will disappoint, neglect, mistreat, and betray us, but the King has kept His word and has never left us. We are motivated by incentive. Beneath our glowing altruism is the manifest human mantra, "What's in it for me?"

The King, on the other hand, has given us everything and promised the victory in exchange for doing the right thing in the world while He watches.

> Do what is right and good in the Lord's sight, so that it may go well with you and you may go in and take over the good land that the LORD promised on oath to your forefathers, thrusting out all your enemies before you, as the LORD said. (Deut. 6:18–19)

You might blame the boss, that impossible customer, or the corrupt system of which you are a cog. You may even wish you never took the job or started the business. You might feel like leaving for greener pastures, but in your heart you know that it is a divine assignment. This means you must stay until the assignment is completed or you have otherwise been released.

What if the CEO of the universe was orchestrating the affairs of your environment in a way to shape you into the image of the King? Could your seeming setback be a setup? For the King cares most about you. He often turns up the heat so that you can see what comes out. Would this knowledge help you to pray for those with whom you work or to be more patient? Can you put away every thought attempting to cast you as the victim and begin walking and talking as the victor?

When the BIB does his work as unto the Lord, the interest in his inheritance account begins compounding. The inheritance is now available to us in the land of the living.

Let us raise the bar in our work. Do it in excellence. Do it in love for those that are privileged to touch the King's ambassador, and, by all means, do it with the joy of the Lord. This is today's divine assignment.

The believer in business has a unique advantage and opportunity to use his businesses as a platform to share the Gospel. We can do good business and contribute to "everyday savings."

Jesus often spoke to the multitude. Today, the multitude is in the marketplace. So much of our time, talent, and resources are spent in the marketplace. Let's establish the marketplace simply as the community of buying, selling, trading, investing, and serving. This community is inescapable for most people. It is retail, wholesale, web-based, mail-ordered, and networked. It is everywhere that value is exchanged for value or promise for promise. We all, at some point, enter the marketplace to acquire what we need, to trade what we have for what we want, or to invest in our futures. We go to the marketplace to work, to shop, to dine, and for recreation. Even when we go without making a transaction we contribute the measurable impact of our steps as traffic that can be translated into future sales.

The multitude is in the marketplace. They are buyers, sellers, and passersby. They are saints, sinners, and backsliders too. They are believers, thinkers, doubters, and haters. They are inquiring souls desiring to fill a need. They are the multitude.

Jesus went to the multitudes to share the good news of the Kingdom's arrival. He went where they were and taught out in the open. He taught among the fishermen, the tax collectors, and taxpayers. While He ministered in the marketplace, He zealously expressed His disdain for making the house of God a place of merchandise (Luke 19:46). This story is not at all a knock on business, but Jesus's clear condemnation on what had been misplaced in what was to be a "house of prayer." Some things and some places must remain sacred. It was not the activity that prompted the only recorded tirade of the Lamb of God; it was the *location* of the activity that provoked Him to turn over the tables.

Believers in Business need a sacred place to join in worship and receive the Word of God. The market is a place that can often breed greed, corruption, and thievery. This amplifies the need for believers to recharge and take their faith to work, in the marketplace and elsewhere. Let us not take the marketplace to the church, but take the church to the marketplace. We are the church! We must seek to infect the marketplace with the righteousness of Jesus.

He is sending you. You will network, meet, greet, negotiate, manage, and motivate many who don't know God's saving grace. You have been commissioned to the marketplace. Some of those you will meet this week in the course of business may never be closer to the Kingdom than they are when meeting with you. Ask Jesus for a way to point them to the Kingdom as you do your business. Ask Him. He will sit in on your meeting. He has already given us the confidence.

> He saw two boats lying on the shore, but the fishermen had stepped out of them and were washing their nets. So Jesus got into one of the boats (the one that belonged to Simon) and asked him to push out a little from the shore. Then he sat down and began to teach the crowds from the boat. (Luke 5:2–3)

Christian business owners have dual-realm authority to proclaim the Kingdom of God where they work. They have the divine decree of wealth-building authority and of private stewardship granted under the law of the land. Both realms coincide in a marketplace enterprise bearing witness to the power and authority to speak forth the good news. There is a gate open to Christian business owners to serve, teach, and direct the employees under their care with time-tested biblical truths. The believer in business may well be the extension of the Ephesians 4:11 ministry gifts in the marketplace. We can become apostles, prophets, evangelists, pastors and teachers where we work. Recent court cases have reinforced the right of an enterprise to hire based on religion and to conduct voluntary Bible studies at work. Owners have rights to share the Gospel within the context of their enterprises. As royal priests, the

BIB has the responsibility to lead others to the Kingdom. They must only demonstrate the faith and resolve to do it.

While some are arguing over Wal-Mart's choice to greet its customers with "Happy Holidays" in lieu of "Merry Christmas," marketplace ministers can lovingly proclaim, "Jesus Christ is Lord." They can print it on every advertisement and every receipt. They can say it to close every transaction with every supplier and every customer. They can flood the marketplace with the love of Jesus and the express power of His name. They can bring all new meaning to the phrase "everyday savings."

We see in Luke 5:1–7 where Jesus is preaching to the multitude on the banks of Lake Gennesaret. As crowds began to press closer, Jesus, having already scanned the environment, looked over and saw two docked fishing boats. He got into one of the boats and asked Simon to push it away from the shore. From this floating platform the Word was preached. When He finished speaking, He asked them to put the boat out into deep water and throw out the nets for a catch. Simon was reluctant and complained, "Master, we have worked all night and caught nothing, but I will do as you say." Simon cast the nets and they filled with fish so much that the nets began to break and the boat nearly sank from the weight of the catch.

Jesus invited Simon to use the tools of his profession to become a platform for the Word. Simon received an abundant blessing. This blessing was the direct result of Simon using his business to support the Word. Then he received the overflow of blessing. The Lord pays for what He orders and He pays back a great return for anything He borrows. Our Christian businesses can support the Gospel with every asset on our books. Offer your conference rooms, your time, talent and treasures. What can you share to promote the Gospel? The Master might be saying, "I have need of this."

Vision

And it shall come to pass afterward, that I will pour out My Spirit on all flesh; your sons and your daughters shall prophesy, your old men shall dream dreams, and your young men shall see visions (Joel 2:28)

A Look at Vision

In the face of devastation, depression, and the deluge of bad news, God's people people need inspiration that motivates them to believe for and strive toward a brighter today. It may seem the media is giving evil more than its fifteen minutes of fame. That's when we need to say more about what we believe and, especially, what we hope to see.

The believer in business must have faith and vision, for we walk by faith and not by sight. We see a greater day in our future, and our hearts must not wait to rejoice. So let us rejoice today. Believers are commanded to show forth His great light in the form of hope, encouragement, and vision for those around us.

We only need to speak forth the truth of what our CEO has already said concerning His people. He says, "For I know the plans I have for you, declares the LORD, plans to prosper you and not to harm you, plans to give you a hope and a future" (Jer. 29:11). In His system He always gives a preview of coming attractions.

What would you do if you knew that you would always win in the end? If you are a believer in business you should DO IT, because your future has already been planned. Don't you wish you could see the future? Not the future from a psychic or other agent of the father of lies, but what if you knew what your Manufacturer has planned for you? Well, believer, you can know because He placed something in your heart.

Our Manufacturer says, "Delight thyself also in the LORD; and he shall give thee the desires of thine heart" (Ps. 37:4).

This doesn't mean that He will deliver toys to our doorstep, but that He placed the desires in our hearts to begin with. It is up to us to breathe them out into our lives in a real and tangible way. Some call it vision, some call it genius, some even call it luck, but believers in business always know the source of our vision. As discussed previously, Biblical Economic Principle 1 is Trust God: our source.

Once again, the basic difference between biblical economics and the secular is conception. The standard definition for economics is the study of production, distribution, and consumption of resources. This definition and, hence, the most broadly understood body of knowledge related to economics ignores the source, the concept that is placed in our hearts by God and later birthed into the time space continuum.

In God's economy, we have to say what we hope to see. This is one of the mysteries of the Kingdom in which we live. Now faith is the stuff of things hoped for, and the proof of the invisible. We have the power of life and death in our tongues. We have direct access to the Creator and CEO of the universe. He is the same one who spoke the earth into existence.

Here's the best part: God the Creator created a creative being to create. What are you prepared to create by speaking it into your business, your ministry, or your life? Fight off that devil in the background that's telling you, "It's not that easy." All great things start with vision. Believe and receive or fight by your own power and might—your choice.

Whether you are a dreamer or a visionary, you will only see what you say. So speak life. Speak of the inspiring future that has been placed in your heart.

> The thing that has been—it is what will be again, and that which has been done is that which will be done again; and there is nothing new under the sun. (Eccles. 1:9)

Vision is an essential skill of the biblical economist. A vision is not about programs or objectives or scenarios or goals. A vision is about seeing in such a way and communicating what you see in a way that other people come to life with new enthusiasm and resolve.

We can depend on the Creator for revelation in the form of witty inventions and concepts to be birthed in our enterprises. The believer in business is always in some stage of the birthing process. He or she often feels some pain and angst connected to dissatisfaction with the current state or an unquenchable passion for a future yet out of reach.

We begin to feel the passion to see restoration, or new provision for those whom we serve. It's not that we are fortunetellers with a crystal ball. It is more often the case that we have a desire to see a need fulfilled, or to bring joy, simplicity, and comfort back into the lives of our loved ones. We just want to help them see.

Recall in John 1:43–51 when Phillip told Nathaniel that he had found Jesus of Nazareth. Nathaniel replied, "Nazareth! Can anything good come from there?" Phillip answered, "Come and see."

This is what visionaries do to help people to see. They help them to see signs of the times, to see their world, to see themselves, to see God, and most importantly to see for themselves.

You might hesitate to believe that everything you have always wanted already exists. All of it exists in eternity, and a great deal of our heart's desire has already existed in time. It has simply been manifest in a different form for a different time. We get goose-pimply when a new product service or even a sermon puts us back in wonderfully familiar emotional state. This is in essence just clever repackaging. Not to suggest that there is no progressive revelation, but to acknowledge that revelation is relative to each individual's enlightenment. Let's help them to see.

Sometimes we can reflect on the wonderful things of the past in order to put our spirits in touch with our heart's desire for right now. Just as God created everything in the very beginning and said of all of it, "That's good," the best that we can aspire to is the restoration to our glorious beginnings. Restoring our lives, our families, and our communities back to their original intent is a future hope based on the glorious past. As Zechariah prophesied,

> Thus says the Lord of hosts: Old men and old women shall again sit in the streets of Jerusalem, each one with his staff in his hand because of his great age. The streets of the city will be filled with boys and girls playing in the streets. (Zech. 8:4–5)

This simple vision of restoration is filled with hope and nostalgic splendor. It portrays trans-generational community of safety, and peace. It speaks of the grandparents and the children, but where are the parents in middle of the day? Perhaps they are working in the marketplace while the seasoned saints and children enjoy the peace of a prosperous community. There aren't enough communities like this anymore, but doesn't it sound like a wonderful place to live? In this community, I might not have to arrange "play dates" for my children. They could go out into the neighborhood and parks and play like we used to.

So, reminiscing can inspire vision. What do you remember that is worth restoring in the world around you? Although as Solomon said, "There is nothing new under the sun," all the ingredients to bring the Kingdom of God into our present reality are already here. So, conceive them, speak them, write them, and bring them to life.

Let us rediscover grand visions and paint a picture that is inspiring, compelling, and clearly communicated. You can help others to see, to hope, and to strive together for a better today.

6

Protocols and Planning

I tell you the truth, anyone who has faith in me will do what I have been doing. He will do even greater things than these, because I am going to the Father. And I will do whatever you ask in my name, so that the Son may bring glory to the Father. *John 14:12–14*

Protocol to Pray

In a Christian business Jesus is regularly acknowledged and consulted. Prayer invites the Lord into a place where He has granted us dominion. Believers in Business must, through prayer, ask the Lord where to cast their nets. This is the key distinction for us. In a Christian business Jesus is the CEO. He has left us in charge to manage. He is only a prayer away when we need Him.

Jesus gives His power to us with an expectation that we would do "even greater." Kingdom delegation of authority requires that we invite His guidance and intervention into our affairs. He gave power to us in the earth to carry out His mission. He is not the kind of boss who gives responsibility without authority. He will not interfere with your affairs until you make a request. This Kingdom protocol is called prayer.

In Jesus's organizational model, He established an enterprise and made disciples, who became apostles. He handpicked twelve. They later picked more, who picked more, who eventually picked someone who prayed you into the Kingdom. We are required to make disciples and lead others to the kingdom. We must multiply ourselves by cultivating persons around us who can carry out the gospel in the context of conducting business.

> You did not choose Me but I chose you, and appointed you that you would go and bear fruit, and that your fruit would remain, so that whatever you ask of the Father in My name He may give to you. (John 15:16)

Christian business begins with prayer. Prayer literally means "request." It's amazing how far a blessing over a meal can go to identify an enterprise as a house of prayer. The multitude is drawn to places of prayer. Many in the marketplace have an empty place in their hearts. If someone would only pray with them, they could see the light. Believers in Business must pray behind the scenes and right out in the open. Pray before the meeting. Pray quietly during the meeting. He's listening. Whether a business owner or one on assignment as an employee, you can establish Kingdom dominion through prayer.

If Jesus is not in your business, is it because you have not invited Him?

Now if you obey me fully and keep my covenant, then out of all nations you will be my treasured possession. Although the whole earth is mine, you will be for me a kingdom of priests and a holy nation." These are the words you are to speak to the Israelites. (Exod. 19:5–6)

Proverbial Economic Planning

Roll your works upon the Lord [commit and trust them wholly to Him; He will cause your thoughts to become agreeable to His will, and] so shall your plans be established and succeed. (Prov. 16:3, AMP)

Take the time to schedule your next economic evaluation. Consider how much of your fiscal year has been spent so far and perform a progress check. It is a good time to reflect, assess, and adjust your plans. Planning is an economic endeavor. It involves projecting a desired state, setting a course, taking action, and assessing results.

According to Noah Webster's 1828 edition of *An American Dictionary of English Language,* an economist is "one who expends money, time or labor judiciously, and without waste." This early definition describes a person that we all strive to become. Not only do we wish to expend without waste, we expect a return. Economists have the peculiar responsibility to predict the future. We may call it projections, forecasts, or even wild guesses, but we have inescapable need to anticipate what's next and take action that positions us to achieve our desired state in that distant future.

We have desires, ambitions, and goals. We devise schemes, and will seek the least painful or most rewarding way to achieve them. It is this instinct that makes us economists, and children of God. Our Creator admires efficiency as well. This explains why He prefers multiplication to addition. He also checks His work. Even as He created the earth, He evaluated each day and concluded, "This is good."

Along the journey to success in business or any worthwhile endeavor, it is important to perform periodic checks on progress. It is part of the direction-setting or strategic planning process. This is an essential economic tool. It is not simply an event, but a regular part of the process to navigate toward your goals.

At the halfway point, let's take a look at your plan's vitals.

- How are your plans progressing?
- Are you on track?
- Have you achieved 25%, 50%, or 75% of the goal(s) (depending on where you are in your fiscal year)?
- What adjustments are needed?

Whether your plans are behind or ahead of schedule, they can be improved with God's guidance. Proverbs 16:3 instructs us to hand over our plans to the Master. It is analogous to a camel that must first kneel and roll over to unload its burden of cargo. It encourages the believer in business to bow our knees and roll our works over to Him. If we lay down our burdens and submit our plans to Him, He will cause our thoughts to become aligned with His will so that our plans will succeed.

The believer in business has a unique advantage in that we have access to the One who knows all things. Our CEO knows and He wants to show us His will. God promises that He will show us the way when we ask.

> Call to me and I will answer you and tell you great and unsearchable things you do not know. (Jer. 33:3)

Planning for the Believer in Business

Prayer – requesting God's direction. He is always present and available for counsel.

Labor – working our measure, putting our hands to the plow. We must do our part.

Anticipation – looking for a return and having great expectations.

Navigation – choosing wisely and according to predetermined course of action

Listen to advice and accept instruction, and in the end you will be wise. Many are the plans in a man's heart, but it is the Lord's purpose that prevails (Prov. 19:20–21).

7

Kingdom Giving

For God so loved the world that he gave his one and only Son, that whoever believes in him shall not perish but have eternal life. *(John 3:16)*

Giving the Perfect Gift

At Christmas, birthdays, and other gift-giving occasions, we often shop or surf the web searching for the perfect gift. Even as believers in business, we are often solicited for contributions to worthy charities and we often give. What rationale do you use for how and to whom you give? Is it who seems most needy, or who asks the hardest, or is it the one that catches you in a moment of benevolence? It is pretty hard to give wrongly unless you are not giving at all. However, there is a more perfect gift.

> Each one should use whatever gift he has received to serve others, faithfully administering God's grace in its various forms. (1 Pet. 4:10)

The truth is that we need not look very far. The perfect gift is the one that the Creator and CEO hid within you. He shaped you into His image that you would be able to serve others. He is most pleased when you are personally congruent and walking in your unique gifting. Too often we fall into the trap of assimilation and emulation of other models of success. The most satisfying and outrageous success will follow self-discovery and actualization. God's grace is the divine ability to be and to do what He intended for you.

Success comes in many forms. It comes in many more shapes, hues, and sizes beyond the iconic, stereotypical Western-European male model of success in business. A diversity of gifts and a multitude of manifestations reflect the genius of God's plan for unity. It is as if He put a piece of Himself in each of us. You can give the perfect gift when you perfect your gift and give it to others.

While giving is good, well-intentioned benevolence does not necessarily offer the best gift. For instance, is it best for a medical doctor to give her unskilled labor to build a house for a needy family or to give free physical exams, or other critical services to those without health care? Is it better for a lawyer to distribute meals at the soup kitchen or to give pro bono legal support to the poor and neglected locked outside the doors of justice? It may feel good, or even offer a good photo opportunity, but it likely is not your best gift.

> Every good and perfect gift is from above, coming down
> from the Father of the heavenly lights, who does not change
> like shifting shadows. He chose to give us birth through the
> word of truth, that we might be a kind of first fruits of all
> he created. (James 1:17–18)

God gave His best, His Son, a part of Himself in order that we
might have everlasting life. He could have chosen other remedies for our
eternal affliction. Perhaps He could have given us Band-Aids, weapons,
or medicine to cover up the pain of sin, and kept His son alive. He
could have watched Jesus marry and have children. God could have
been a grandpa! No, He gave His perfect Son at the perfect time for the
strategically perfect cause—to save us all for eternity! Is it too much to
ask that we strive to give our best gifts?

> In everything I did, I showed you that by this kind of hard
> work we must help the weak, remembering the words the
> Lord Jesus himself said: 'It is more blessed to give than to
> receive. (Acts 20:35)

While being generous, be strategic about giving. Consider what
charities most need what you have to offer. Then give them your best.
This might include serving on boards and committees. It might mean
giving your highly marketable services away to a needy person or cause.
It might mean that you give access to your facilities, capital, or other
infrastructure for the sake of advancing a worthy Kingdom mission.

Ask the Lord to lead you to the right strategic charity so that you
can give your perfect gift.

Avoiding the Holiday Hangover

> Let no debt remain outstanding, except the continuing debt
> to love one another, for he who loves his fellowman has
> fulfilled the law. (Rom. 13:8)

For many Believers the Christmas season is filled with busyness in shopping, preparing, fellowshipping, and setting themselves up to begin the new year with unwanted credit card debt.

I could talk for pages about the real meaning of Christmas and how consumerism has exploited a well-intentioned tradition. I could even regale you on the not so subtle Keynesian influences cajoling us to think that rampant retail spending in the last five weeks of the year will somehow save our economy from a recession. Keysenian economics, founded by John Maynard Keynes is the foundation for western economics as we have learned it. It emphasizes short term thinking and is hence contrary to the biblical view of leaving and inheritance to our children's children.

Instead we will take a more practical view of avoiding economic traps during the holidays. Whether you celebrate Christmas, Hanukah, Kwanza, the winter solstice, or Fred Claus Day, unless you are in hibernation between Thanksgiving and New Year's Day, your spending will likely increase. So, please indulge me to share a handful of wise, prudent and practical economic sense.

In 2016, shoppers around the country say they are planning to spend an average of $929 for gifts this holiday season, up from $882 last year according to the 32nd annual survey on holiday spending from the American Research Group, Inc. That equates to over 20 percent of the median gross monthly income for a family of four ($48K). With the US savings rate slightly negative, therefore, many families' festivities will be paid for well into next year.

Your traditions and spending plan may be just fine, but perhaps someone you know could be blessed by your sharing a few economic truths concerning the holidays. To that end we are providing a few suggestions to consider that might help someone avoid the holiday debt hangover.

1. Choose your holiday traditions prayerfully and thoughtfully, especially young families. You can begin creating your own, keeping some old and creating new traditions that fit your family vision. It's harder to fire Santa than to have never brought him onto the family's annual payroll.

2. "See to it that no one takes you captive through philosophy and empty deception, according to the tradition of men, according to the elementary principles of the world, rather than according to Christ" (Col. 2:8).

3. Make a holiday spending plan. Decide how much you can comfortably spend on gifts and celebrations this year. If gifts are a part of your tradition, make a list of all the people to whom you would like to give gifts. After completing your list, write down how much you would like to spend on each person. Be sure to include the costs of decorations, wrapping, cards, and extra groceries in your spending plan.

4. Give good memories. Take a trip; plan some quality time with your beloveds. Keep in mind that some of the most appreciated gifts are not those that cost the most money but are the most meaningful. Handmade gifts, such as calendars, photo albums, and framed children's artwork can provide a lifetime of smiles. Give your time and service to those in need. And never underestimate the power of a sentimental letter, song, or poem for that special person on your list. These heartfelt gifts are often the perfect choice.

5. Pay it forward by earning extra income to finance your holiday purchases. Many retailers need seasonal help to accommodate holiday shoppers. Taking a part-time job on the weekends will let you earn enough cash to avoid financing your purchases with credit cards.

6. Leave your credit cards at home. Studies have shown that people who use credit cards to buy gifts spend an average of 30 percent more than people who use cash. When you add in all the finance charges over months, or even years, that "perfect gift" could cost you twice what you paid for it, or more.

The holiday season is great for family, fun, and festivities. It need not be a drain on our finances. Never let twelve months of good stewardship go down the drain in December. You are blessed to be a blessing and chosen to lead by example. I pray you receive this and pass it on in the spirit of getting understanding.

It is still better to give than to receive, and while this may the season for giving, our best is to give love on Christmas and every other day.

"But the angel said to them, 'Do not be afraid; for behold, I bring you good news of great joy which will be for all the people'" (Luke 2:10).

A Kingdom Key: Giving Thanks in Advance.

> Then He ordered the crowds to recline on the grass; and He took the five loaves and the two fish, and, looking up to heaven, He gave thanks and blessed and broke the loaves and handed the pieces to the disciples, and the disciples gave them to the people. (Matt. 14:19, AMP)

So many things in the Kingdom of God are directly opposite to that of the world system. It is as if when God said that He made us in His image, He made us His reflection in a glass. Therein left is right, right is left, trying to save your life is to lose it, letting go is the best way to keep the ones you love, etc. Similarly is the principle of thanksgiving. In the biblical economy we give thanks in advance. Instead of just giving thanks for what we have been given, giving Him thanks for what He is yet to give often results in your receiving what you have faithfully hoped for.

Taking a critical look at each miracle of Jesus feeding a multitude, we see Him giving thanks in advance. A conventional reading of the passage above would assume Jesus gave thanks for the small portions that He had in inventory. But which thoughts were likely more prevalent in His mind: the little in hand or the abundance to come? Most likely, He was giving thanks in advance for the coming overflow of fish and loaves. This faithful appreciation for the yet-to-come opened the heavens for the miraculous. Jesus was modeling for us faithful thanksgiving in advance.

Giving thanks in advance makes it hard for a loving, generous Father to say, "No." I have heard it said that you must become grateful before becoming great. To give thanks is appreciation. When you appreciate something or someone you increase its value. So, to appreciate your business, your employees, your customers' satisfaction increases their value and better enables their increase to abound to your account.

Imagine for a moment your little child crawling up in your lap and saying, "Mom (or Dad), I just want to thank you for taking me for ice cream later today." You might think that was really cute. Odds are you will take the kid for ice cream. The thanksgiving increased your value and afforded you to give out of your heart. This is how thanksgiving in advance works with our Father.

Having a genuine attitude of gratitude is a strategic asset for the believer in business. It follows the law of attraction. You will attract the things that you truly appreciate. Your "pre-appreciation" attracts success. Success is looking for a place to land, a place to increase. If your heart is filled with gratitude, then success will seek you out.

> His master said to him, Well done, you upright (honorable, admirable) and faithful servant! You have been faithful and trustworthy over a little; I will put you in charge of much. Enter into and share the joy (the delight, the blessedness) which your master enjoys. (Matt. 25:21)

The wise stewards took what the Master gave them and appreciated its value. They showed their gratitude in advance of His return. So He shared His joy, delight, and blessedness.

It is still a good thing to give thanks in retrospect so that we never forget the source of all we have, but try seasoning all your petitions with thanksgiving and see if you experience a greater measure of success.

> Do not fret or have any anxiety about anything, but in every circumstance and in everything, by prayer and petition (definite requests), with thanksgiving, continue to make your wants known to God. (Phil. 4:6)

Take a few minutes to thank God for what He has already done for you. Then make a list of your biggest hopes and prayers—the ones that you have been praying about, and the ones you may have been too afraid to even ask for. This time go to Him and thank Him in advance for making your BHAGs (Big Hairy Audacious Goals) come true.

"At all times and for everything giving thanks in the name of our Lord Jesus Christ to God the Father" (Eph. 5:20).

8

The Big 10

Remember this: Whoever sows sparingly will also reap sparingly, and whoever sows generously will also reap generously. Each man should give what he has decided in his heart to give, not reluctantly or under compulsion, for God loves a cheerful giver. *2 Corinthians 9:6–7*

Believers in Business often ask, "Should I be tithing from my business?" This is a loaded question because it is chocked full of assumptions. It might mean, "Should I take 10 percent of my sales and give it to the church?" Or "Should I take 10 percent of my profits and give to a worthy charity?" Or better yet, "Am I obliged to pay 10 percent of anything anywhere?" Let's provide a simple guide, and then move on the weightier matters.

Think of your business as the machine that makes dough. If the machine makes 1one hundred pounds of dough, you may or may not have 10 percent of the dough left over after you've paid the lease, raw materials, the wages, utilities, and taxes. Whatever is left over after these commitments are honored is your profit. As the sole proprietor, you can take all the extra dough home to trade it for groceries. This is the dough you ought to base your giving percentage on. In the same way, if you are an employee earning a paycheck, you would return 10 percent of your gross check amount to the CEO of the universe. You can give more from your business, but don't be confused about being scripturally obliged to do so.

Woe to you, teachers of the law and Pharisees, you hypocrites! You give a tenth of your spices-mint, dill and cumin. But you have neglected the more important matters of the law-justice, mercy and faithfulness. (Matt. 23:23)

The heart condition behind the giving is paramount. A mite given in sacrificial love is more valuable to God than a billion dollar tithe given out of compulsion. We can sometimes tithe our way into pride. It is not enough to pay 10 percent to please God; it is the heart condition that matters most. The rich young ruler in Luke 18:12 boasted of paying a tenth of all he possessed and yet, he still was not saved.

Christians should abandon the idea of paying a tithe and put on the desire to give generously from the heart. If Christians were faithfully taught to give to the Lord with all their heart and to excel in their giving, church contributions and individual acts of benevolence would rise rather than decline. Analogous to one's personal savings, there is no prescribed upper or lower limit, but good stewards strive to save as much as possible. Christian giving ought to have the same character of excellence that is demonstrated by more generous giving.

Liberty from law or simply from oppressive doctrine is not an excuse for the believer to give any less than s/he is currently giving (tithes and offerings) to a church. Freedom should allow us to give even more. Abandoning religious routine, Christians should seek the Lord for guidance as to where, how much, and to whom we give. We should always give prayerfully, generously, and faithfully to our churches, to charities, and to those in need. As Lord Acton said, "Liberty is not the power of doing what we like, but the right of being able to do what we ought" (Ballor, 2013).

Is Tithing for Christians?

> A tithe of everything from the land, whether grain from the soil or fruit from the trees, belongs to the LORD; it is holy to the LORD. (Lev. 27:30)

Let us be lovers of understanding and truth. Let the truth make us free. We have the need to spread the good news of the Kingdom of God and the knowledge of His system of economics. So, we will dare to share the history, various points of view on this topic and finally converge on spiritually discerned and wisely thought-through perspective to the question, "Is tithing for Christians?"

Many Christians believe in giving 10 percent of their income to the church as a faithful duty or obligation. This law-based approach is common among many denominations. The contemporary principle-based point of view preached by biblical economists, such as the late Larry Burkett, espouse the validity of the tithe principle as an effective means of ensuring the continuance of blessings and protection from the devourer, but they maintain that tithing is completely voluntary (Burkett, 2000). There is another deeply staked camp of opinion that is convinced that tithing income is just flat wrong, unscriptural, misinterpreted in the Old Testament, and not relevant in the New Testament (Fiedler, 2000). Where did Christians get the idea to tithe? Who is right? Moreover, what is the responsibility of Christian[s] regarding financial support for the local church and other worthy causes?

A "tithe" comes from the Hebrew word *mah-as-ar'* (Strong, 1995) that literally means "a tenth part." The practice of tithing predates the Mosaic Law and is not unique to the Judeo-Christian faith. In Lydia, a tithe of cattle was offered to the gods; the Arabians paid a tithe of incense to the god Sabis; and the Carthaginians brought tithes to Melkarth, the god of Tyre. The explanation of why a tenth was chosen among so many different peoples is said to be that mystical significance of the number ten. Ten denotes the perfection of divine order, the capacity and responsibility of man. The number 10, it was thought, signified totality, for it contains all the numbers that make up the numerical system, and indeed all imaginable series of numbers, and so it represents all kinds of property, which was perceived to be a gift of God (Johnston, 1990).

The traditional practice was to submit 10 percent of one's land, produce, or increase to a higher priest. The biblical Old Testament describes this law, but the New Testament contains only four references to tithing (Matthew 23, Luke 11, Luke 18, Hebrews 7). Tithing (a verb) is translated in contemporary Christian dogma as the requirement to give or "pay" 10 percent of one's income to the local church from which a person receives spiritual teaching. It is the requirement to pay 10 percent of either the gross or net income of a family to a church organization. Doctrine and application vary across Christian denominations, especially regarding whether it is more appropriate to pay a tenth of gross or net income.

Before we do the arithmetic, let us first determine whether giving 10 percent of your income to the Church is a divine requirement.

> Will a man rob God? Yet you rob me. "But you ask, 'How do we rob you?' In tithes and offerings. You are under a curse-the whole nation of you-because you are robbing me. Bring the whole tithe into the storehouse, that there may be food in my house. Test me in this," says the LORD Almighty, "and see if I will not throw open the floodgates of heaven and pour out so much blessing that you will not have room enough for it." (Mal. 3:8–10)

Robbers or Rabbis, Curses or Christ?

Malachi 3 is often used as the favorite dogmatic rationale for tithing. It is often used to evoke fear in the believer. The prophet's admonishment of the priests for bringing lame and diseased animals as sacrificial offerings is often taught as a "tithe or else" command from God. The promise to "pour out a blessing" and to keep the devourer from one's resources is taught as God's covering of property insurance for those who tithe. Alternatively, those who don't tithe are robbing God and, therefore, are cursed with a curse.

Even though Malachi's admonishment is directed at the priests, verse 9 indicts the entire nation for robbing God. The challenge for the New Covenant believer is to determine whether or not this law of blessing and bane applies today. Nobody wants to be cursed. Malachi, the last book of the Old Testament, records the prophet's admonishment for repentance in the area of tithing and other sins. Could the Old Testament finale offer instruction in anticipation of the New Covenant? Or was it merely another illustration of the inadequacy of the law?

So what about the curses in Malachi? What curses? The Bible does not offer any punishment for failure to tithe. Malachi 3:10 does proclaim curses over Israel at that time. Is there any reason to assume the curse applies to believers today? God spoke to them in the present concerning the actions in their past. So I cannot be cursed because He was not talking about me. If God had said, "I will curse the perpetrators who don't do this," then perhaps it would apply to believers today. Moreover, Jesus's complete work redeemed me from the curse.

Read Galatians 3:13: "Christ redeemed us from the curse of the law by becoming a curse for us, for it is written: 'Cursed is everyone who is hung on a tree.'"

It is not good hermeneutics to take a prescription or command in one instance and apply it to all present and future cases. This is much like the Christian socialists' interpretation that states when Jesus instructed the rich young ruler to sell all his possessions and give them to the poor that He spoke condemnation against wealth. It was the prescription for one man's blind, idolatrous materialism. Likewise, the condemnation of Israel in Malachi was for that people. Not to imply that these instances are not instructive; they are. It is simply that they don't alone establish a universally applicable principle.

There is more good news here. God did not project the curse in the future-continuous tense, but He did project the blessings of obedience into the future when He says,

"Test me in this," says the LORD Almighty, "and see if I will not throw open the floodgates of heaven and pour out so much blessing that you will not have room enough for it. I will prevent pests from devouring your crops, and the vines in your fields will not cast their fruit" says the LORD Almighty." (Malachi 3:10-11)

God says, "I will, if you will." He spoke a promise here in the future-continuous tense for those who will test Him concerning giving a tenth. So, not only am I not cursed, but best of all I still have access to the blessings of giving a tenth should I choose it. This sounds like an incredible deal. It sounds like grace—getting better than I deserve.

The Early Church and Tithing Paradigms

The early Church had no tithing system. The tithes of the Old Testament were regarded as abrogated by the law of Christ... But as the Church expanded and its material needs grew more numerous and complex, it became necessary to adopt a definite rule to which people could be held either by a sense of moral obligation or by a precept of positive law. The tithing of the Old Law provided an obvious model, and it began to be taught. The Council of Macon in 585 ordered payment of tithes and threatened excommunication to those who refused to comply (Fanning, 1912).

Despite the contestable appropriateness of the monetary tithe doctrine in the New Testament Church, the practice should make economics considerably easier for the pastor, administrator, and church board. In theory, they can count on using the heavy fiat of God to obligate their congregants to pay a fixed percent of incomes. It is treated as a non-negotiable act of obedience. This should make a good portion of the churches' financial support predictable and automatic. Ironically, only 20 percent of Christians in tithe teaching churches pay tithes (even in churches that teach it as a requirement). Despite the pervasiveness of this doctrine, Christians in general give on average 2–3 percent of their income (Ronsvalle & Ronsvalle, 2001). This begs the question: Is mandatory giving the best way to increase contributions to the Church?

So why is giving so low in a system of mandatory 10 percent payments? There is a threshold of faith for the modern-day Christian, especially in the United States where people are comfortable attending church and volunteering for church activities. Yet many have not really surrendered their lives and, much less, their wallets over to the Lord. Perhaps more importantly, the mandatory payment conflicts with the spirit of love and grace of the New Covenant. It is the Lord's desire that each person gives as he or she is able (Deut. 16:17 and 2 Cor. 9:7). Forcing what was meant to be given in love corrupts the gift. God wants His children to give cheerfully, joyfully, and with pleasure, not out of fear or obligation. Yet when the motivation is to avoid the pain of a curse, it breeds fear. Fear opposes faith and, thus, breeds rebellion, and rebellion, enmity with God in the form of humanistic materialism. Giving will increase with a greater acknowledgement of the liberty in Christ. When we replace fear with faith, we will see an outpouring of generous grace giving.

The table below summarizes three common paradigms relating to tithing.

Summary of Tithing Paradigms

Summary of Tithing Paradigms	Traditional Law Based	Contemporary Principle Based	Grace Giving
Doctrinal View	To tithe is to obey. Anything else is rebellious and subject to curses.	Tithing is voluntary and good to do.	Tithing has been taught in fear
Notable Proponents	Kenneth Copland; T.D Jakes; Reconstructionists – North, Jordan	Larry Burkett, Carson	Webb, Fielder
Key Rationale	Literal interpretation of certain Old Testament scriptures.	Abrogation of the law	Abrogation of the law Tithe was not money
Scriptural Summary	Leviticus 27:30 Malachi 3:10 Hebrews 7:9	Deuteronomy 16,17 2 Corinthians 9:6-9	Matthew 5:17-18 John 1:17 Mark 12:29-34
Dogma	"The capitalization of all life is made possible when the tithe is properly paid and directed"	Tithing was always a voluntary act	The command to give to the poor is most important
Emphasis	Obligatory 10% to the church before offerings are acceptable	Support for the local church through tithes and offerings	Individual Christian grace giving along with the responsibility to support ministry and the poor
View on Alternatives	There is no prosperity without tithing	Others just need to be taught	Misguided traditions

The Reason We Give: Giving Is for Christians

> This is how we know what love is: Jesus Christ laid down
> his life for us. And we ought to lay down our lives for our
> brothers. If anyone has material possessions and sees his
> brother in need but has no pity on him, how can the love of
> God be in him? (1 John 3:17)

Now, how should a God-fearing, obedient, free-willed Christian give
faithfully and wisely?

Fortunately, within Paul's teachings to the early church, the Bible
is pretty clear on how to give and the purposes for giving. Second
Corinthians 9:6–9 provides a superb capsule of the appropriate attitude
toward Christian giving:

Remember this:

> Whoever sows sparingly will also reap sparingly, and who
> ever sows generously will also reap generously. Each man
> should give what he has decided in his heart to give, not
> reluctantly or under compulsion, for God loves a cheerful
> giver. (2 Corinthians 9:6-7)

Jesus came to preach the good news to the poor, to proclaim freedom,
recovered sight, release from oppression, and to declare a season of the
Lord's favor (Luke 4:14). Each person claiming to belong to Christ,
calling himself or herself Christian, must, therefore, exist for this same
reason. Each group, ministry, fellowship, or other form of organization
calling itself Christian must, too, subscribe and act to fulfill the same
purpose. Christian giving must be in the context of this new freedom.
It must demonstrate our recovered sight concerning God's pleasure.

Christians should give because it pleases God. It is one of the ways
we demonstrate our faith, obedience, and, most importantly, our love
for the Lord.

> So we make it our goal to please Him, whether we are at
> home in the body or away from it. (2 Cor. 5:9)

And we pray this in order that you may live a life worthy of the Lord and may please him in every way: bearing fruit in every good work, growing in the knowledge of God, being strengthened with all power according to his glorious might so that you may have great endurance and patience, and joyfully giving thanks to the Father, who has qualified you to share in the inheritance of the saints in the kingdom of light. (Col. 1:10)

God loves or is pleased by a cheerful giver. Love, in this instance, is the Greek word *agapao* (ag-ap-ah'-o). It means "to be pleased with a person." The Amplified Translation renders 2 Corinthians 9:7 as follows:

He takes pleasure in, prizes above other things, and is unwilling to abandon or to do without a cheerful, and prompt to do it giver whose heart is in the giving.

It pleases God to see His children give from the heart. He prizes such a giver above a religiously ardent tithe payer. As the New Testament has God's law inscribed on our hearts, He is more pleased by a loving action that comes from the heart than an act of conformity to rules on paper or spoken from the mouths of humans. The mark of the true Christian is love demonstrated in self-sacrifice and practical charity as expressed in 1 John 3:11–18. Loving God is demonstrated by our giving to one another.

The care and comfort of the needy ought to be a focal point Christian fellowship and especially Christian giving. The Bible is replete with points emphasizing concern for the poor. In the Old Testament landowners were expected to leave an amount from the harvest to be gleaned by the poor. Several regulations addressed fair treatment of the poor. Jesus regularly emphasized giving to the poor as He thrice recommends that goods be sold and given to the poor. He said that we would always have the poor among us. The need to aid the poor is patently obvious in today's bimodal world economy. In most nations of the world, the distribution of wealth is characterized by a few very rich and a large and growing poor. Christian giving to the poor is essential to fulfilling Jesus's commission to the saints.

9

On Wealth and Abundance

Zaccheus stopped and said to the Lord, "Behold, Lord, half of my possessions I will give to the poor, and if I have defrauded anyone of anything, I will give back four times as much." And Jesus said to him "Today salvation has come to this house, because he, too, is a son of Abraham. For the Son of Man has come to seek and to save that which was lost."

—Luke 19:8–10

When the believer in business begins to seek the preponderance of marketplace keys within scripture, we will increase our effectiveness in His great commission and release blessings into our homes and businesses. Luke 19 is an example of marketplace manna that illustrates the inextricable link between the Kingdom of God and the marketplace. This chapter includes Zaccheus's conversion, the parable of the ten minas, Jesus's triumphant entry to Jerusalem, and His classic cleansing of the temple.

In Luke 19:8, Zaccheus pledged half of this wealth to the poor and set up an escrow account to repay anyone who had lost money in dishonest dealings. Jesus declared Zaccheus's entire household saved, including his small-office-home-office (SOHO) enterprise. For in these times, perhaps for different reasons than today, many businesses operated out of the home. This enabled the children to be trained in family business, which integrated the work and family into a harmonious balance. Jesus acknowledged that this Israelite household, and all within it, was being restored to the covenant with his forefather Abraham.

Then Jesus went on to say something that seems somewhat out of place. He stated His purpose for coming. "For the Son of Man has come to seek and to save that which was lost." What motivated Jesus to make this statement? Could it be that Zaccheus's conversion and economic restoration provided a metaphor for what Jesus came to do?

To gain more insight into what Jesus was saying, we must determine what "that which was lost" is. What did Jesus come to seek and save? What was lost when sin entered in?

In the beginning we lived in a place named Eden—translated "pleasure." We had daily communion with God. The economy there was one of abundance. Everything we needed had already been provided for our consumption. And we lived in perfect harmony with each other. This is that which was lost. Jesus came looking for and endeavoring to restore communion with the Father, the abundant life and harmonious living to the children of God. Is Jesus letting us know that He came for more than to save souls? He wants to see us living in pleasure as it was in the beginning. His encounter with Zaccheus, a sinner seeking Christ, provides an illustration of the transaction of faith and Kingdom restoration. One marketplace sinner accepting Jesus multiplied blessings and ushered in right standing with God.

Then, because the listeners were eager to see the appearance of the Kingdom of God, Jesus launched into the parable of the minas. This parable, like the parable of the talents, demonstrates God's intention for us to take what He gives us and multiply it. In this familiar parable, the nobleman greatly rewards the profitable servants and strips the unprofitable one. He redistributes wealth to the faithful and gives them charge over cities.

So, we are to seek a return to communion with God, an economy of abundance and harmony with our brethren. What better place to seek this than in the marketplace. In the marketplace we will find an abundance of opportunities to create value, a multitude of relationships needing to be harmonized and a loving God waiting to be invited into your office, boardroom, or power lunch.

Camels and Frappuccino

> Then Jesus said to his disciples, "I tell you the truth, it is hard for a rich man to enter the kingdom of heaven. Again I tell you, it is easier for a camel to go through the eye of a needle than for a rich man to enter the kingdom of God." (Matt. 19:24)

This is often a challenging passage for the believer in business. It is often avoided, misinterpreted, or watered down in clever sermonizing. It is challenging because many of us have an unfettered desire to be a wealthy Christian. Jesus makes a rather clear allegory using commonly understood objects from the marketplace of His time. In today's vernacular, He might have said, "It is easier to drive a Hummer® through a Starbucks Frappuccino®." Whatever the subjects of the allegory, it is clear that He meant to convey that it is exceedingly difficult for a rich man to enter the Kingdom of God. Many of us secretly wish He meant something else, but our simple hermeneutical guide would suggest an interpretation based on the rule, "if a literal interpretation makes good sense, then interpret it literally." So let us conclude that Jesus meant what He said.

Many of us have heard the story that Jesus was not referring to a real needle, but He was referring to a poorly designed passageway through the Jerusalem city wall. The city engineers had not considered the girth of a fully loaded camel. So the camel would have to lay down its baggage and drop to its knees in order to get through. While this is the raw material for an awesome sermon, scholars have failed to find any evidence of such a doorway. This brings us back to the simple idea of an exceedingly large object passing through an exceedingly small opening and, therefore, a rich man stuck outside the Kingdom of God.

There is more good news. Jesus went on to say, "With men it is impossible, but with God all things are possible." I would much rather go through the eye of a needle or even drive through a frappuccino with God. He makes it so that entry to the Kingdom requires surrender to the King. I am so grateful Jesus was clear that we cannot get to the Kingdom of our own strength, religious zeal, financial acuity, or self-righteousness. It will never be good enough just to be a good person.

While the example of the rich young ruler was an example and object lesson, Jesus was not making him the rule. He was not teaching us that every person desiring salvation must sell all they have and give it to the poor. He was teaching us that those who hold on to what they have more tightly than their love for the Kingdom of God and His righteous shall never find it. In the same way that Abram had to be willing to sacrifice his only begotten son, we have to be willing to relinquish our belongings and aspirations in order to enter His kingdom.

The fact is that "Rich" was not really surprised. Although he was religious enough to have tithed and kept all the commandments since the time of his youth, he somehow knew in his heart that he was still lacking something. He knew of his own avarice and love of money. Perhaps he hoped that Jesus would overlook it just to have him join the congregation.

Jesus does not require us to be poor. He wants to love us and pour His goodness upon us. He became poor so that we don't have to.

> For you are becoming progressively acquainted with and recognizing more strongly and clearly the grace of our Lord Jesus Christ (His kindness, His gracious generosity, His undeserved favor and spiritual blessing), [in] that though He was [so very] rich, yet for your sakes He became [so very] poor, in order that by His poverty you might become enriched (abundantly supplied). (2 Cor. 8:9, AMP)

Remind yourself that Jesus wants to see you abundantly supplied. Then tell somebody. Maybe they will ask, "What must I do to be saved?"

Salvation is free, yet it will cost you everything.

Keys to Kingdom Abundance

> The knowledge of the secrets of the kingdom of heaven has been given to you, but not to them. Whoever has will be given more, and he will have abundance. Whoever does not have, even what he has will be taken from him. (Matt. 13:12)

Jesus gives the keys to abundance. So believe in His word and expect more in faith. Abundance in the Greek is *persseuo,* meaning "super abounding quantity or quality, superfluous, in extraordinary excess." Matthew 13:11–12 makes four assertions:

1. There is a Kingdom.
2. It has secrets.
3. Knowledge of the Kingdom leads to abundance.
4. Ignorance (not having the knowledge) leads to lack.

- There is a kingdom in heaven. The King came to earth to make a proclamation. He said, "Turn around, you are going the wrong way, the Kingdom of Heaven is coming here." He came to fulfill a mission to establish the Kingdom of heaven in the earth. The message for that mission is the Gospel. The Good News is "The Kingdom of heaven is here." He came just to say, "The Kingdom is now in the earth."
- This is the only message He came to deliver. It was not to build a church, not to be baptized, not to reap and sow, not to pay tithes. It was not to speak in tongues. The message was not to learn the Ten Commandments or the 613 laws of the Bible. It was not how to obtain wealth to some 30, 60, and 100-fold. While these things are important for believers, we must

understand that they were not our Savior's principal message. He did not need to preach a prosperity message because kings already own everything. His message was simply, "I've got some good news. THE KINGDOM IS BEING RESTORED IN YOUR MIDST! The Kingdom of God is here!"

- Understanding the concept of Kingdom may be a bit challenging for those of us living in a republic. Royal sovereignty is something that we associate only with fairy tales. We associate kings and queens with fables such as *Cinderella, Snow White, The Prince and the Pauper,* and *The Princess Bride.* The media effectively reduces the issues of royalty such as Queen Elizabeth, Prince Charles, and Lady Diane to tabloid entertainment.
- Here a few Kingdom principles:

  o   Kings are born, not elected.
  o   Kings are kings for life.
  o   The King's decrees are permanent.
  o   The King owns everything in the Kingdom.

The earth is the Lord's, and everything in it. He is Lord, and owner, and possessor of it all. We don't often think of the Lord as our owner. Yet, we are familiar with the term "landlord." This describes an owner, or lord of the land. Lords can give any portion of what they own to anyone they chose. They often give to their children. In the beginning God, the Father, was the king. Adam, His creation, had right standing with the King. As kings do, God bequeathed dominion over the entire territory of the earth to Adam (Gen. 1:26–28). He gave His son a planet. He's the Landlord and He can do that.

After receiving this incomparable gift, Adam surrendered his dominion to the enemy. Adam's offspring continued to act in rebellion until they got bold enough to make a formal request to separate from the Kingdom. Their declaration of independence is in 1 Samuel 8:4 where they requested a king like all the other nations. This was a clear rejection of God's sovereignty.

Jesus came to restore the Kingdom, to restore man's right standing, and to restore the Holy Spirit within the man. He was part of the Master's plan. Jesus tells us in Luke 22:29-30 "And I appoint unto you a kingdom, as my Father hath appointed unto me." As a born-again, spirit-filled believer, you have been given a Kingdom.

Are you walking in your royal privilege?

Marketplace Meekness

> Blessed are the meek, for they will inherit the earth (Matthew 5:5)

We are instinctively wired to survive, think, and find the best way to meet our desires. We have learned to strive, to fight, and to negotiate life in our favor. Then when Jesus says that the meek will get the prize, it puts us on our heels for a moment. Is our Lord directing us to be weak, spineless pushovers?

Despite the typical short-term horizon that typifies the prevailing economic philosophy of our time, most can align their motivations with the idea of receiving an inheritance. An inheritance is a future reward that is more based upon who you are than what you have done. This inheritance is not in heaven, but here in the Kingdom of Heaven in the earth. The notion of an inheritance places you in a much-improved economic position. Inheriting the earth or land grants you one of the two essential elements of wealth. To some degree, we all want wealth. Even the most humble has the inner desire to see the fruit of their efforts providing a future harvest of benefits.

In business the iconic success model is self-interested, aggressive, and driven to success. He may even dance along the slippery slope of ethics, law, and greed. Hence the notion of meekness as it is generally interpreted is as far away from this persona as Pharaoh is from the altar call. How does the believer in business strive for good success, possess the land, and yet be meek enough to receive the promised inheritance?

The meek are those who are kind, gentle, humble, patient, mild, and long-suffering. The Bible offers innumerable reinforcements that God provides grace and favor to those exemplifying these qualities. The temptation is great to be selfish, mean-spirited, and impatient. The world offers many reinforcements that such qualities pay better wages, especially in the short term. Meekness is not weakness. It requires more strength and intestinal fortitude to refrain from retaliation than to succumb to the reflex to strike back. This strength enables us to produce lasting success while preserving relationships and sharing the wealth. Perhaps Bill Gates and Warren Buffett are today's best role models in this respect. These two of the world's most wealthy are said to be gentle, kind, humble, and extremely generous.

Let's look at Moses, the deliverer, and the man who opened the door to the Promised Land. Exodus 2:3 says, "Now the man Moses was very meek (gentle, kind, and humble) or above all the men on the face of the earth."

We are all too familiar with Moses's strength and great exploits, but we rarely think of him as meek. This characterization was in the context of his receiving attacks from his sister and brother about his choice of an Ethiopian wife. They not only challenged his judgment, they challenged his authority. Moses, in his steely meekness, did not defend either. God spoke on his behalf, and affirmed his unique relationship with Moses and struck both friendly firers with leprosy. Yet, due to his meekness, Moses interceded on their behalf and delivered them from a certain and painful death.

> He leads the humble in justice, And He teaches the humble His way. All the paths of the LORD are lovingkindness and truth. To those who keep His covenant and His testimonies. For Your name's sake, O LORD, Pardon my iniquity, for it is great. Who is the man who fears the LORD? He will instruct him in the way he should choose. His soul will abide in prosperity, And his descendants will inherit the land. (Psalm 25:9–13)

There is little room in business to be passive or apathetic with respect to planning, acting, and trading value in the marketplace. We must allow the Lord to teach us in His way. His Holy Spirit will lead us into all truth, and show us where to cast our nets, feed our cattle, and where to possess the most fertile pastures. We can achieve business success and inherit the land through "marketplace meekness"—a strength to do business God's way.

> But the meek will inherit the land and enjoy peace and prosperity. (Ps. 37:11)

10

Business Cycles and Seasons

He changes the times and the seasons; He removes kings and sets up kings. He gives wisdom to the wise and knowledge to those who have understanding! He reveals the deep and secret things; He knows what is in the darkness, and the light dwells with Him!

—*Daniel 2:21–22*

With latest news in the financial markets, our economy is being defined by the network of conversations attempting to speculate what will happen next. Pundits ponder and pontificate their projections for the economy's future. Who really knows? What is certain is that seasons change constantly. For the astute person in business, the horizon never moves; there is only the amplitude of the waves. Success is not forever, and failure is not fatal. In all things, we must take some solace in the knowledge that this too will pass.

> "There is an appointed time for everything. And there is a time for every event under heaven- A time to give birth and a time to die; A time to plant and a time to uproot what is planted" (Eccles. 3:1–2).

Economists study trends and cycles attempting to predict, plan, and prepare for what's next. Believers in business must do the same. However, we have access to the One who knows all things. Will He tell you which strategy to pursue?

He told Peter exactly where to throw his nets before they overflowed with fish (Luke 5:4–7). He told Nehemiah what to say to ensure the funding of his urban redevelopment project (Neh. 1:11, 2:4). He told Jeremiah to purchase blighted property in his hometown of Anathoth while it was yet behind enemy lines in anticipation of its future restoration (Jer. 34:6). He really does want to direct our paths when we acknowledge Him in all our ways. If you believe He will, ask Him and He will tell you too.

If you've been in business for anytime or if you plan to stay, you will face crises. There are times when the cycles of life and business put us on the precipice of entrepreneurial peril. There are times when the euphoria of success coaxes us to ride with our hands in the air. These are times when we are compelled by the rush of gravitational force to call on the CEO of the universe for help, peace or the strength to endure. It is in these troughs that we learn of our deep and spiritually rooted resilience. Faced with the essential yet still surprising truth, that I am yet alive sparks every neuron and awakens the spirit of omniscience within our souls. The question so patently apparent—what do I do now?

If you keep your head up and knees bowed you can use the counsel of the Most High God to navigate the cycles of economic contraction and growth. Down times are often the best times to sow into your future. Unlike the typical investor who follows the hot market tips and consequently buys high and bales low, the wise economist is buying when the multitude is selling. Even if it's not necessarily a time to make purchases, it is an opportune time to retool, read or reread, refresh, and ready yourself for the frantic pace of the imminent upturn in activity.

The Lord is not a fortuneteller, but He did give us this promise in Jeremiah 33:2–3: Thus says the LORD who made the earth, the LORD who formed it to establish it, the LORD is His name, "Call to Me and I will answer you, and I will tell you great and mighty things, which you do not know."

The Lord is the answer to all things. As Daniel 2:21–22 points out, He reveals the deep and secret things. He knows what is in the darkness (the unknown and seemingly unknowable). The light (knowledge and wisdom) dwells in Him. I think I will just ask him.

How about today you invite Him to sit in your business chair and set His course for your good success in the coming economic change. No appointment necessary.

In the Long Run, We Live Forever

> Then Jacob called for his sons and said: "Gather around so I can tell you what will happen to you in days to come. Assemble and listen, sons of Jacob; listen to your father Israel."
>
> All these are the twelve tribes of Israel, and this is what their father said to them when he blessed them, giving each the blessing appropriate to him.
>
> (Gen. 49:1, 28)

Israel possessing the full promise of the Abrahamic Covenant is transferring the blessings to his next generation. Picture a scene from a who-done-it movie where the patriarch has gathered all the children together to tell them how they will be bequeathed within his last will and testament. Now, place that scene in an era that wealth and provision was held entirely within the construct of the family or clan. Every family has some form of business. There are no corporations or sole proprietorships outside of the family. This is a time wherein faith, family, and finances are inextricably linked.

This adds context to the original derivation for the term economics. Recall that it is derived from the Greek word *okionomia,* meaning "the law of the household." Elements of the economy such as seedtime and harvest may seem obvious, but even more so were the essential customs of generational blessing and wealth transfer. The house of Jacob, which became the house of Israel, had responsibility for distributing all the Promised Land to its next generation. You can bet this was an all-important, dramatic, and suspense-filled gathering.

Israel was giving each child a blessing appropriate for his service, honor, and obedience. One might wonder if everyone at the meeting was in touch with the fact that results of the meeting were determined long before. Perhaps every invitee is running the mental tapes of their past choices, their relationship with their father, and whether they will receive a blessing or bane.

Similarly, for us, the decisions we make today can affect us for many years to come. Life is only short in the grand scheme. For instance, fifty years is a long time in the span of one's life. That's how long we may have to live with a bad choice made in our youth. Not only can today's decisions affect us for the balance of our lives, they can affect the generations that come long after us.

The problem is that we are bombarded with the short-term, microwave mentality. We have subconsciously bought into the notion that everything needs attention right now. Our addiction to immediate gratification has diminished our ability to wait, think it over, and act wisely. It has filled every single minute with some distraction. Short-term thinking and nonstop working have become our societal norms. This underlying philosophy is covertly undermining our ability to apply the keys to the Kingdom and receive the blessings of the Father.

This same philosophy epitomizes the Keynesian economic paradigm. John Maynard Keynes, the reputed father of modern macroeconomics, espoused a disdain for the long-term view. He felt strongly that the long-term view was worthless. He is remembered for his quip, "In the long run we are all dead." As his biographer Robert Skidelsky noted, Keynes's had a "lifelong bias against long-run thinking" and "He was not prepared to risk too much of the present for the sake of a better future."

The biblical economy is framed by cycles, seasons, and transitions. It is a system based upon a long-term orientation. The Father makes this clear in of the Ten Commandments. The only commandment with a promise tells us that in order to live long, we must honor our parents. And the commandment that He wanted to make doubly sure we don't forget is the one that begins with "Remember the Sabbath." He wants us to remember that in His divine plan there are cycles and seasons, days for work and days for rest. Together they say, "Honor your parents and live long, and as long as you live, remember to rest in Me."

The long run is now here. As Proverbs 13:22 says, "A good man leaves an inheritance to his children's children."

Reflections

1) What has been or yet can be imparted to you from your parents?
2) What will you impart to the next generation?
3.) What decisions must you make today to insure a good inheritance for your grandchildren?

"I will establish my covenant as an everlasting covenant between me and you and your descendants after you for the generations to come, to be your God and the God of your descendants after you" (Gen. 17:7).

Standing Firm While He Does the Shaking

> This is what the Lord Almighty says: 'In a little while I will once more shake the heavens and the earth, the sea and the dry land. I will shake all nations, and what is desired by all nations will come, and I will fill this house with glory,' says the Lord Almighty. 'The silver is mine and the gold is mine,' declares the Lord Almighty. The glory of this present house will be greater than the glory of the former house,' says the Lord Almighty. 'And in this place I will grant peace,' declares the Lord Almighty.
>
> (Haggai 2:6-9)

While our Creator and CEO is astonishing, awesome, and faithful to do exceedingly abundantly above all we can ever ask or think (Eph. 3:20). He is not a God of surprises. He is consistent in the way in which He warns people of His Kingdom what to expect. He sends his prophets to point the way and implores those who have ears to hear. He told Israel of the coming blessings for the house of Israel. As they came out of exile, God was preparing to fulfill his promises to them, but He wanted them to return to obedience and the work of building the house of God.

"The silver is mine and the gold is mine," declares the LORD of hosts. "The latter glory of this house will be greater than the former" says the LORD of hosts, "and in this place I will give peace," declares the LORD of hosts. (Hag. 2:8)

This passage from Haggai is a timely one for this season. The prophet Haggai was sent in connection with the Feast of Ingathering. The name Haggai is derived from the Hebrew word *hag*, meaning festive. Scholars suspect that he was born on the day of a major feast such as Tabernacles. Whether legend or coincidence concerning his birthday, Haggai's second encouragement, from which this passage is taken, was spoken as part of the great feast. He rebukes Israel for losing focus on God and the completion of the physical temple, but his words also prophesied the coming Messiah and greater temple of the living God.

This prophetic message was revelatory for the people in 520 BC and likewise for us today. God is reminding us not to despise small beginnings. He is calling us to reflect upon the blessings of old and the splendor of the past house. Moreover, he encourages us not to languish in the disappointments of our present accomplishments, but to strive together toward a brighter and grander future, for the latter (what is to come) shall be greater than the former. He reminds them in verse 2 of the promise He made as He brought them out of the Egyptian system. I have learned that whenever God says "Do not fear," this means that somebody or something is attempting to make me afraid. Vis-à-vis sensationalized gloom and doom predictions on the economy, the believer in business must decide whose report to believe. We need not take counsel from those in the news or popular press concerning our provision, success, or even what strategies to implement. The believer in business must seek the face of the Father to hear the word of feast, famine, or anything in between. We remain bullish, as we keep our heads up in the midst of discouraging economic commentary. Often God asks His children to do great things in the seemingly least opportune time, and clearly at odds with conventional wisdom. So we stand firm while He does the shaking. We stand firm on His promises.

Our expectations for good success must be re-rooted in His covenantal promises. Be encouraged today for your Father is about to do some shaking.

Will you be in position to gather what falls?

Reflections

1. Are you willing to believe that your promises are yet secure in Him?
2. What word has He given you?
3. What are you building for the glory of God?
4. Can you still see it as big, or as impactful as when you first conceived it?

Read the short, power-packed Book of Haggai this week and keep building!

Summary of Biblical Economic Principles Table 1

Name	Principle
1. Trust God	**God is the source, arbitrator and rewarder of all wealth.** • He gives the power to obtain wealth (Deut 8:18) • He is a rewarder of those who diligently seek Him (Hebrews 11:6) • Blessed is the nation whose God is Yahweh (Psalm 33:12) • "If they (the righteous) obey and serve Him, They shall spend their days in prosperity, And their years in pleasures" (Job 36:11).
2. Manage Wisely	**Humans are the stewards of God's good abundant earth.** • "and God blessed them and said to them, 'be fruitful, multiply and replenish...'" (Gen 1:28) • "The earth is the Lord's, and everything in it (Prov 24.1)
3. Be Responsible	**Each individual person is given the opportunity for stewardship and the accountability for the disposition of resources.** • "You have been faithful of little, so I will make you master over much (Matthew 5:21) • "Didn't it belong to you before it was sold? And after it was sold, wasn't the money at your disposal?" (Acts 5:3-4)

| 4. Do What You Do Best (work your measure) | **Each individual is called to reflect God's creative nature through the application of human capital (ingenuity, labor) to creation.**
• But to each one of us grace has been given as Christ apportioned it. (Ephesians 4:7)
• For you created my inmost being; you knit me together in my mother's womb. I praise you because I am fearfully and wonderfully made; your works are wonderful, I know that full well (Psalm 139:13-14)
• The man who plants and the man who waters have one purpose, and each will be rewarded according to his own labor. For we are God's fellow workers; you are God's field, God's building. (1 Corinthians 3:8-9) |
| 5. Sow & Reap | **Each individual is given the right and obligation to work and productively share in God's provision for their basic needs of food, shelter, and clothing.**
• "Then the Lord took Adam and put him in the garden to dress and to keep it." (Gen 2:15)
• "In the sweat of your face you will eat bread (Gen 3:19)
• '…if anyone is not willing to work, then he is not to eat either" (2 Thessalonians 3:10)
• There is nothing better for a man than to eat and drink and tell him that his labor is good. This also I have seen, that it is from the hand of God (Ecclesiastes 2:24) |

Summary of Biblical Economic Principles Table 2

Name	Principle
6. Collaborate	**Social cooperation in the form of work is essential to prosperous stewardship.**

- From him {Christ} the whole body, joined and held together by every supporting ligament, grows and builds itself up in love, as each part does its work (Ephesians7:21).
- If one part suffers, every part suffers with it; if one part is honored, every part rejoices with it. Now you are the body of Christ, and each one of you is a part of it (1Corinthians 12:26).
- Again, I tell you that if two of you on earth agree about anything you ask for, it will be done for you by my Father in heaven. For where two or three come together in my name, there am I with them (Matthew 18:19-20)

Name	Principle
7. Respect Private Stewardship	**Private ownership and access to the means of production is essential to the achievement of economic freedom and therefore Human freedom.**

- For every breach of trust, whether it is for ox, for donkey, for sheep for clothing or for any lost thing, both parties will come before the judges" (Exodus 22:9).
- You shall not move your neighbors landmark (Deut 19:14).

**8. Give
Opportunity**

Economic efforts of one must not deprive others of their rights as stewards.

- Do not charge your brother interest, whether on money or food or anything else that may earn interest (Deuteronomy 23:19)
- Let us not become weary in doing good, for at the proper time we will reap a harvest if we do not give up. [10] Therefore, as we have opportunity, let us do good to all people, especially to those who belong to the family of believers. (Galatians 6:9-10)
- When you reap the harvest of your land, do not reap to the very edges of your field or gather the gleanings of your harvest. Leave them for the poor and for the foreigner residing among you. I am the LORD your God.(Leviticus 22:23)

**9. Give to the
Needy**

Stewardship includes the responsibility to produce sufficient provision for the marginalized and the poor.

- Those who oppress the poor insult their Maker, but those who help the poor honor him (Proverbs 24:31)
- He that giveth unto the poor shall not lack: but he that hideth his eyes shall have many a curse. (Proverbs 28:27)
- (As it is written, He hath dispersed abroad; he hath given to the poor: his righteousness remaineth for ever. (2 Corinthians 9:9)

**10. Respect the
Law of the
Land**

Government's role is to protect the rights of private ownership and to provide the balance of justice between work and wealth.

- Everyone must submit himself to the governing authorities, for there is no authority except that which God has established. The authorities that exist have been established by God (Romans 13:1).

Notes

"32d annual survey on holiday spending." American Research Group, Inc. Last modified November 21, 2016. https://americanresearchgroup.com/holiday/.

Ballor, Jordan J. "Lord Acton on Catholic and Modern Views of Liberty | Acton PowerBlog." Acton Institute PowerBlog. Accessed November 29, 2016. http://blog.acton.org/archives/57615-lord-acton-on-catholic-and-modern-views-of-liberty.html.

Burkctt, Larry, and Randy Southern. *The World's Easiest Guide to Finances.* Chicago: Northfield Pub, 2000.

Croteau, David A., Ken Hemphill, Bobby L. Eklund, Reggie M. Kidd, Gary North, and Scott M. Preissler. *Perspectives on Tithing: 4 Views.* Nashville, Tenn: B & H Academic, 2011.

Fanning, W. H. W. "Tithes (Anglo-Saxon teotha, a tenth)." *The Catholic Encyclopedia* Volume XIV, no. July 1 (n.d.), 174-175.

Fiedler, Sandy. "TITHE? GIVE? -- WHAT SHOULD I DO?" Welcome to Studies in Reformed Theology. Last modified 2000. http://reformed-theology.org/html/issue10/tithe.htm.

Friesner, D. N. "Book Review: Shakespearean Tragedy: Its Art and its Christian Premises." *Christianity & Literature* 19, no. 2 (1970), 22-27. doi:10.1177/014833317001900211.

John Paul II. "Encyclical Letter CENTESIMUS ANNUS." Vatican. Accessed March 7, 2002. http://www.vatican.va/holy_father/john_paul_ii/encyclicals/index.htm.

Johnston, R. D., R. D. *The Numeral Ten, Numbers in the Bible (pp. 79)*. Grand Rapids:: Kregel, 1990.

Jordan, James B. "The Law of the Covenant. Appendix C: Tithing." In *Small Collections*. 1986. http://www.wordmp3.com/details.aspx?id=13689.

Kendall, R. T. *Tithing, a Call to Serious, Biblical Giving*. Grand Rapids, Mich: Zondervan Pub. House, 1983.

Mandino, O. *The greatest secrets of success*. Chicago, IL: Og Mandino, 1990.

The Matrix. Directed by The Wachowski Brothers. 1999. Warner Brothers, Film. After Neo has been reborn into truth, He asks' Why do my eyes hurt?" Morpheus, a type of John the Baptist replies, "they have never seen before."

North, Gary. *An Introduction to Christian Economics*. [Nutley, N.J.]: Craig Press, 1973.

Patton, Judd W. "Is There a Christian Political Economy." *Journal of Interdisciplinary Studies* 3, no. 1/2 (1991).

Ronsvalle, John, and Sylvia Ronsvalle. "Rediscovering accountability." *New Directions for Philanthropic Fundraising* 1997, no. 17 (1997), 45-62. doi:10.1002/pf.41219971706.

Shank, Duane. "Faith-Based Discrimination? Religious Organizations and Fair Hiring." *Sojourners Magazine*, October 2003.

Silvoso, Ed. "Introduction." In *Anointed for Business*. Ventura, Calif: Regal, 2002.

Skidelsky, Robert. "Reply." *Keynes as Philosopher-Economist*, 1991, 139-141. doi:10.1007/978-1-349-10325-6_10.

Sowell, Thomas. "1." In *What is Economics. In Basic Economics: A Citizen's Guide to the Economy.* New York: Basic Books, 2000.

Stebbins, J. M. "Business and the Common Good." *Social Responsibility, Entrepreneurship and the Common Good*, Fall 1997. doi:10.1057/9780230354890.0006.

Tiemstra, John P. "Christianity and Economics: A Review of Recent Literature." *Christian Scholars' Review* 22, no. 3 (1993), 227-247.

Vanderheyden, Terry. "Wal-Mart Replaces Christmas with 'Happy Holidays': Catholic Civil Rights Group Launches Boycott." *LifeSiteNews.com* (NEW YORK), November 10, 2005.

Webb, Michael L., Mitchell T. Webb, and Sharon Y. Brown. *Beyond Tithes & Offerings.* Tacoma, WA: On Time Pub, 1998.]

Edwards Brothers Malloy
Ann Arbor MI. USA
March 9, 2017